Th

MW00986309

The
Green Bible
Devotional

A Book of Daily Readings

by Carla Barnhill

HarperOne
An Imprint of HarperCollinsPublishers

Bible quotations, unless otherwise noted, are from the New Revised
Standard Version of the Bible, copyright © 1989 by the Division of Christian Education of the National Council of Churches of Christ in the U.S.A.

THE GREEN BIBLE DEVOTIONAL: *A Book of Daily Readings.* Copyright © 2009
by HarperCollins Publishers. All rights reserved. Printed in the United
States of America. No part of this book may be used or reproduced in
any manner whatsoever without written permission except in the case of
brief quotations embodied in critical articles and reviews. For information
address HarperCollins Publishers, 10 East 53rd Street, New York, NY
10022.

HarperCollins books may be purchased for educational, business, or sales
promotional use. For information please write: Special Markets Department,
HarperCollins Publishers, 10 East 53rd Street, New York, NY 10022.

HarperCollins Web site: http://www.harpercollins.com

HarperCollins®, �®, and HarperOne™ are trademarks of
HarperCollins Publishers.

Special thanks for advisory review to Calvin B. DeWitt
and Lowell (Rusty) Pritchard.

FIRST EDITION

Library of Congress Cataloging-in-Publication Data

Bible. English. New Revised Standard. Selections. 2009.
    The Green Bible devotional : a book of daily readings / edited by Carla
Barnhill. — 1st ed.
        p. cm.
    ISBN 978–0–06–188585–3
    1. Human ecology—Biblical teaching.   2. Human ecology—Religious
aspects—Christianity—Meditations.   I. Barnhill, Carla.   II. Title.
BT695.5.B537   2009
242'.5—dc22   2009020272

© **Mixed Sources**
Product group from well-managed
forests, controlled sources and
recycled wood or fiber
FSC www.fsc.org Cert no. SCS-COC-00648
© 1996 Forest Stewardship Council

09 10 11 12 13   RRD(H)   10 9 8 7 6 5 4 3 2 1

We give you thanks, most gracious God, for the beauty of the earth and sky and sea; for the richness of mountains, plains, and rivers; for the songs of birds and the loveliness of flowers. We praise you for these good gifts and pray that we may safeguard them for our posterity. Grant that we may continue to grow in our grateful enjoyment of your abundant creation, to the honor and glory of your Name, now and forever.

—*The Book of Common Prayer* (1549)

Contents

Air

Animals

Humanity

Stewardship

Introduction

Green living. Green cleaning. A green office. It's clear that the word *green* has become the buzzword of current pop culture. Green ideology has gone from a fringe movement among neo-hippies to a full-bore societal priority, one touted by the government and big business alike. But for those who have long advocated for the environment, there is concern that this broader interest in the earth is little more than a trend, one that will fall by the wayside when the next new thing comes along.

Communities of faith have had a rather tumultuous relationship with the environmental movement. For every Christian who has found resonance with the idea of creation care, there are three more who believe it borders on idolatry. Some believe we are called to care for this earth; others believe this earth is meant to decay before we can see the return of Christ and his kingdom. Some believe God is active and present in nature; others believe that recognizing God's glory in the wind and the trees borders on pantheism. Some have been eager to join in with the new wave of environmental activism; others have rejected talk of creation care, suggesting that pagan influences are infiltrating the church. These divisions have left many people of faith wondering just where God's people ought to stand when it comes to caring for the environment.

Yet the Bible leaves little question as to the position into which God's people are called. The daily devotions that follow will take you on a journey through the Bible, one that moves from the Creation story in Genesis to the Revelation to John of the new heaven and the new earth. Whether you are new to the faith, new to the creation care conversation, or living an integrated life in both, here you will find insights into God's relationship with the earth, the waters, the air around us, the animals, and all of humanity. And you will discover how clearly God has called us to care for what God has made.

In her essay in *The Green Bible*, theologian Ellen Davis writes:

> *Being fully human means also understanding our unbreakable bond with the land, that material base of life. One cannot go more than a few chapters in the Old Testament without seeing some vivid reference to land and its importance for humanity, beginning with the image of* adam *(Heb., "man, humankind") formed from* adamah *("soil") in Genesis 2:7. That wordplay suggests a kind of familial connection; it is a subtle yet powerful reminder that the life of a people comes from its land. We belong to the fertile earth more than it can ever belong to us.*

That unbreakable bond has too often been stretched thin by human indifference. But it's not too late for us to return to the relationship for which God created us. For those who hold an inherent sense that human beings are connected to the earth in a profound way, these readings will ground that belief in God's truth. For those who hold a belief that we are created to live as God's people on this earth, these readings will illuminate what that means for our relationship with all of creation. And for those who remain uncertain as to the call of God's people, these readings will point the way toward a life that is integrated with all that God made.

The daily readings in this devotional are by no means an exhaustive study of the biblical understanding of creation care. But they will give you an overview of what the Bible has to say about humanity's relationship with the rest of God's creation. Each reading includes a passage of Scripture, a short meditation to help guide your thinking on the passage, a prayer, and space for your reflections where you can journal; draw; or paste a photo, leaf, or other reminder from nature. Use these daily readings as a starting point, a place to consider how the biblical message of creation care might play out in your life. Most of all, use them to deepen your understanding of the beautiful interdependence God designed in creation and the vital role you play in the relationship between our Creator and his creation.

Earth

I want creation to penetrate you with so much admiration that wherever you go, the least plant may bring you the clear remembrance of the Creator . . . One blade of grass or one speck of dust is enough to occupy your entire mind in beholding the art with which it has been made.

—Basil the Great (329–79),
  Hexaemeron, Homily V,
  "The Germination of the Earth"

Earth: The Provider

In one way or another, God provides all that we need to
live on the earth—plants and animals for food, fibers for
clothing, clay and stone and wood for shelter. At the dawn of
Creation, it was the earth that stood as the perfect expression
of God's love and care for humanity. There was a garden filled
with fruit, an ocean filled with fish, a sky filled with light.
There was no human need that could not be met through
God's creation. And then God handed it over to humanity,
asking that we till the fields and care for the animals and
have dominion over all that God created. There was a perfect
interdependence between humanity and the earth—as
humans cared for the earth, the earth would care for us.

The ancient Israelites understood this interdependence.
Faith was not something that existed in theoretical realms.
Their faith was earthy, rooted in the common experiences
of daily living. It was not a separate part of life, but a fully
integrated practice that impacted the way people lived and
interacted with creation. The Old Testament is filled with
references to nature. There are rules about planting fields
and caring for livestock. There are prophecies about natural
catastrophes, a result of human disobedience. And there
are astonishing images of the profound goodness of God
demonstrated through the earth's provision. There was a

relationship between human beings and the earth that echoed their relationship with God.

Today, few of us live lives that are connected to the earth. We buy food from grocery stores rather than farmers; we eat fruits and vegetables all year regardless of the growing seasons; we prefer cheap food over ethical practice. Perhaps as we've lost touch with the rhythms of the earth, we have lost touch with that connection to the God who made it as well.

Throughout the Bible, it is clear that God loves the earth and all that is in it. As you read through the passages in this section, notice the depth of God's love for creation. Look for the many ways creation points God's people back to their Creator. Notice how all of creation is included in God's redemptive work. As you do, you will see that this earth, the one we inhabit, is God's home as well.

Explore: Sometime over the next ten days, take a hike in the woods, sit in a green space in the city, or visit a public garden. Find some token of nature from your time outdoors to keep in your home as a tangible connection to the earth on which we live.

God's Presence All Around

The heavens are telling the glory of God;
and the firmament proclaims his handiwork.
Day to day pours forth speech,
and night to night declares knowledge.
There is no speech, nor are there words;
their voice is not heard;
yet their voice goes out through all the earth,
and their words to the end of the world.

—Psalm 19:1–4

Meditation

If you've ever gazed into a star-filled sky or listened to rain
drumming on the roof of a cabin or felt the wind cool your
face, then you have felt what it is like to be in the presence
of God. The earth reflects God's love for creation. It is a
reflection of the One who created it. Each tree and leaf and
rock and bird and child bears the imprint of the artistry
of God. That's why the Psalmist can speak so poetically of
the ways in which the world reflects God's glory. When we
look, when we listen, when we open our hearts to God's
presence, we can't help but see that the whole earth draws
us closer to our Creator.

Prayer

Great God, everything you made points us back to you.
Help us to see your workmanship in the glorious earth
you have made. We do not worship the creation, we
worship you, the Creator, and yet we know that you have
surrounded us with your beautiful earth so that we might
never fail to recognize your presence and the wonders of
your creation.

Reflection

Ultimate Power

The voice of the LORD is over the waters;
the God of glory thunders,
the LORD, over mighty waters.
The voice of the LORD is powerful;
the voice of the LORD is full of majesty.
The voice of the LORD breaks the cedars;
the LORD breaks the cedars of Lebanon.
He makes Lebanon skip like a calf,
and Sirion like a young wild ox.
The voice of the LORD flashes forth
flames of fire.
The voice of the LORD shakes the wilderness;
the LORD shakes the wilderness of Kadesh.
The voice of the LORD causes the oaks to whirl,
and strips the forest bare;
and in his temple all say, "Glory!"

—Psalm 29:3–9

Meditation

There are Christians who resist getting involved in creation care because they fear it leads to idolatry, that the earth becomes a kind of god. But this passage makes it clear that sensing God in creation, being aware of God's providence as we care for the earth around us, is not idolatry. It is a recognition of God's power, God's goodness, and God's ultimate role as Creator, Redeemer, and Sustainer. The Psalmist speaks of God's glory revealed in the midst of a storm, that God is bigger than the wind or the water or the thunder or the trees. The poet's vision of God—who is both deeply involved in creation and yet far bigger than creation—is one we can hold on to as well. It is a vision of God who is personal, and it is a vision of how we can know God even more intimately through his creation.

Prayer

Dear Lord, we know that your creation is a picture of who you are. Show us your glory in the world around us. Let the earth be a means for us to draw closer to you as we recognize the wonders of your creation in the air around us, in the water that sustains us, and in the vast resources your earth provides us.

Reflection

The Earth and Its Fullness

"All things are lawful," but not all things are beneficial. "All things are lawful," but not all things build up. Do not seek your own advantage, but that of the other. Eat whatever is sold in the meat market without raising any question on the ground of conscience, for "the earth and its fullness are the LORD's." If an unbeliever invites you to a meal and you are disposed to go, eat whatever is set before you without raising any question on the ground of conscience.   —1 Corinthians 10:23–27

Meditation

This short quote is part of Paul's letter to the church at Corinth. In it, Paul is trying to help the earliest Christians sort out the ins and outs of how they are to live as God's people. Paul spends some time trying to help them establish some basic ground rules so that the different ethnic groups can overcome their differences to live as one church. But what he comes down to is something from an ancient Psalm: "The earth is the Lord's and all that is in it" (Ps 24:1). Because God declared all of creation good there is no reason for food or land or resources to become points of contention among God's people. All of the earth is good. All of creation is good. This is what God said. This is how we need to live.

Prayer

Loving God, you made the earth and everything in it. It all belongs to you. Make us mindful of how we are to live with care and respect for the earth you made and for the lives it sustains.

Reflection

The Voice of the Earth

As he was now approaching the path down from the Mount of Olives, the whole multitude of the disciples began to praise God joyfully with a loud voice for all the deeds of power that they had seen, saying, "Blessed is the king who comes in the name of the LORD! Peace in heaven, and glory in the highest heaven!" Some of the Pharisees in the crowd said to him, "Teacher, order your disciples to stop." He answered, "I tell you, if these were silent, the stones would shout out."

—Luke 19:37–40

Meditation

As Jesus faced those who opposed him, he reminded them of the totality of God's providence. It was not only Jesus who reflected God's presence; it was the earth itself. The earth points to its Creator. The earth, made by the hands and the breath of God, bears testimony to the One who made it. When Jesus was crucified, Luke tells us that the sun itself failed (Lk 23:45). Creation was affected by the death of God's Son and is responsive to its Creator. The very cycle of life and death that is so evident in creation was upended by the resurrection. As the rocks cry out, as the sun goes dark, as death becomes life, nature testifies to the power of God.

Prayer

Creator God, your earth shows us who you are. You are
powerful like the rush of water down a mountain. You are
gentle like a stream trickling through the forest. You revive
us like rain over dry ground. Help us to listen as the rocks
cry out your praises.

Reflection

The Song of the Earth

Praise the LORD!
Praise the LORD from the heavens;
praise him in the heights!
Praise him, all his angels;
praise him, all his host!
Praise him, sun and moon;
praise him, all you shining stars!
Praise him, you highest heavens,
and you waters above the heavens!
Let them praise the name of the LORD,
for he commanded and they were created.
He established them forever and ever;
he fixed their bounds, which cannot be passed.
Praise the LORD from the earth,
you sea monsters and all deeps,
fire and hail, snow and frost,
stormy wind fulfilling his command!
Mountains and all hills,
fruit trees and all cedars!
Wild animals and all cattle,
creeping things and flying birds!
Kings of the earth and all peoples,
princes and all rulers of the earth!
Young men and women alike,

old and young together!

Let them praise the name of the LORD,

for his name alone is exalted;

his glory is above earth and heaven.

He has raised up a horn for his people,

praise for all his faithful,

for the people of Israel who are close to him.

Praise the LORD!

—**Psalm 148:1–14**

Meditation

This glorious Psalm calls on the whole of creation to offer praise to God. There is joy, honor, exaltation in every stanza of this song. But this is not simply a poet's over-the-top expression of worship. It is a recognition of the ways in which creation sings God's praises each day. As the sun comes up and warms the earth, as the rain falls and renews life, as the winter covers the earth in quiet calm, as the spring arrives to remind us of the victory of life over death, all of creation *does* tell the story of God. The joy of the Lord is all around us on God's great earth. When we care for the earth, when we notice God's hand in its cycles and seasons, we are praising our Creator.

Prayer

Almighty God, we praise you for your glorious works, and for how the earth you created feeds us and clothes us and provides for us. Help us to praise you with our hands and our minds and our hearts as we work to protect all that points us to you.

Reflection

A Day of Rest

But if you will not obey me, and do not observe all these commandments, if you spurn my statutes, and abhor my ordinances, so that you will not observe all my commandments, and you break my covenant . . . I will devastate the land, so that your enemies who come to settle in it shall be appalled by it. And you I will scatter among the nations, and I will unsheathe the sword against you; your land shall be a desolation, and your cities a waste. Then the land shall enjoy its sabbath years as long as it lies desolate, while you are in the land of your enemies; then the land shall rest, and enjoy its sabbath years. As long as it lies desolate, it shall have the rest it did not have on your sabbaths when you were living on it.   —Leviticus 26:14–15, 32–35

Meditation

The concept of a true Sabbath—a day of no work—is one that few Christians today can grasp, let alone manage to live out. We consider our lives too busy, our work too demanding to put everything aside and take a day off. But God didn't make the Sabbath optional; it's a command. Yet God's command that we rest isn't just for our benefit. It is meant to give the whole of creation time to recover from the stress we put on it as we go about our daily lives. In Exodus 23:10–11, God lays out a command for letting the earth—the fields, the orchards, the vineyards—rest every seven years. The ground needed time to restore itself so that it could continue to produce good food. And in this passage, God is clear that ignoring that command will bring ruin to the earth and therefore to God's people. If the people wouldn't give the earth its Sabbath, the earth would take it one way or another, in this case while the people were living in exile. Once again, the disobedience of God's people brings about natural consequences. When they fail to live as God commanded them to, ruin comes to the earth and to their lives. Today, few of us are in a position to let our land lie fallow every seven years. But we can help heal the earth by taking one day a week to reduce our use of the earth's resources. For one day each week, we can refrain from using our cars, whittle our water usage to zero, avoid using electricity. And as the earth recovers, we might find that something in us is restored as well.

Prayer

Great God, we have taxed ourselves and your creation beyond our limits. Give us the strength to rest, the power to slow down, the will to relax. Let us be agents of healing and restoration as we allow the earth to rest with us. And as we rest, turn our eyes and hearts to you. Help us find meaning not in activity but in your peaceful presence.

Reflection

Disobedience and Devastation

If you will only obey the LORD your God, by diligently observing all his commandments that I am commanding you today, the LORD your God will set you high above all the nations of the earth . . . But if you will not obey the LORD your God by diligently observing all his commandments and decrees, which I am commanding you today, then all these curses shall come upon you and overtake you: Cursed shall you be in the city, and cursed shall you be in the field. Cursed shall be your basket and your kneading-bowl. Cursed shall be the fruit of your womb, the fruit of your ground, the increase of your cattle and the issue of your flock. Cursed shall you be when you come in, and cursed shall you be when you go out. The LORD will send upon you disaster, panic, and frustration in everything you attempt to do, until you are destroyed and perish quickly, on account of the evil of your deeds, because you have forsaken me. The LORD will make the pestilence cling to you until it has consumed you off the land that you are entering to possess.   **—Deuteronomy 28:1, 15–21**

Meditation

There are long passages throughout the Bible that expand on this idea of God punishing humanity's disobedience through nature. Here, Moses lays out a devastating picture of the cost of rebellion—the earth will become our enemy. God created humans to live as a harmonious part of the created order, as the caretakers of all that God made. When we as human beings forget that calling, the earth pays the price. Famine, drought, disease—these are not part of God's intentions for the earth. They are what come from human selfishness and greed. When we pollute the air, the rain becomes toxic. When we pollute the water, the earth becomes toxic. When we pollute the earth, the earth's resources become toxic. And when the earth suffers, people suffer. Our disobedience brings about devastation.

Prayer

Forgiving God, we confess that we have not cared for the earth as you have called us to. We have failed to love your creation as you do and have ignored the calling to live as your people in the land you gave us. By your grace, heal us of our shortsightedness, our selfishness, our ignorance. Restore in us a vision of partnership and interdependence with all of creation.

Reflection

The Cost of Neglect

The nations raged, but your wrath has come, and the time for judging the dead, for rewarding your servants, the prophets and saints and all who fear your name, both small and great, and for destroying those who destroy the earth.   —**Revelation 11:18**

Meditation

In the midst of the wrath and destruction in the early parts of the revelation to John, we see that humanity's failure to care for creation—for the air, for the water, for the land, for the people—is our great sin. Because all of creation belongs to God, its desolation at our hands is the ultimate sign of our rebellion against God. From the moment humans first turned away from God in the Garden to this vision of destruction, humanity has put itself first and allowed the rest of creation to suffer the consequences. There is no mistaking God's anger over this rebellion. And yet it's not too late for us to step back into God's intentions, to take the call of stewardship seriously, to make ourselves part of what God is doing to bring about a new heaven and a new earth.

Prayer

All-knowing God, we have failed utterly. Forgive us for
the destruction we have brought about over generations
of neglect and selfishness. Show us how to be part of
what you are doing in the world. Inspire us to reclaim
our calling to care for your earth as an act of worship and
praise to you.

Reflection

The Fullness of Restoration

I consider that the sufferings of this present time are not worth comparing with the glory about to be revealed to us. For the creation waits with eager longing for the revealing of the children of God; for the creation was subjected to futility, not of its own will but by the will of the one who subjected it, in hope that the creation itself will be set free from its bondage to decay and will obtain the freedom of the glory of the children of God. We know that the whole creation has been groaning in labor pains until now; and not only the creation, but we ourselves, who have the first fruits of the Spirit, groan inwardly while we wait for adoption, the redemption of our bodies.

—Romans 8:18–23

Meditation

There is something profoundly beautiful about this image of all of creation—the water, the sky, the earth itself—alive with the anticipation of renewal. As we see the decay and destruction that has fallen on the earth through human carelessness, we can be reminded that this is not the end of the story. Instead, all of creation is in the birthing process, holding our collective breath as we labor for new life.

Prayer

Dear Lord, you created all things and redeem all things. We pray for the earth, for the whole of creation, as together we work for the day in which all things will once again be brought to life and wholeness in you. Give us the will to be agents of your healing and redemption—for ourselves and for the blessed world in which we live, now and forever.

Reflection

The Mercy-Filled Earth

Then the LORD became jealous for his land, and had pity on his people. In response to his people the LORD said: I am sending you grain, wine, and oil, and you will be satisfied; and I will no more make you a mockery among the nations. I will remove the northern army far from you, and drive it into a parched and desolate land, its front into the eastern sea, and its rear into the western sea; its stench and foul smell will rise up. Surely he has done great things! Do not fear, O soil; be glad and rejoice, for the LORD has done great things! Do not fear, you animals of the field, for the pastures of the wilderness are green; the tree bears its fruit, the fig tree and vine give their full yield. O children of Zion, be glad and rejoice in the LORD your God; for he has given the early rain for your vindication, he has poured down for you abundant rain, the early and the later rain, as before. The threshing floors shall be full of grain, the vats shall overflow with wine and oil. I will repay you for the years that the swarming locust has eaten, the hopper, the destroyer, and the cutter, my great army, which I sent against you. You shall eat in plenty and be satisfied, and praise the name of the LORD your God, who has dealt wondrously with you. And my people shall never again be put to shame. You shall know that I am in the midst of Israel, and that I, the LORD, am your God and there is no other. And my people shall never again be put to shame.   —Joel 2:18–27

Meditation

So often the prophetic words of the Bible are black-and-white absolutes: humans stray and God pours out wrath. But here, Joel gives us a picture of God's love for humanity, as God anxiously waits for humanity to turn back to him. Forgiveness and grace come swiftly as humanity again follows God. And they come in the form of blessings from the earth—grain and grapes and oil, the return of green fields and the end of plagues, peace to the people. When we follow the way of God, when we live out our call to care for God's creation, our reward is life as God intended, a life of abundant goodness.

Prayer

All-powerful God, we know that you can alter the planet with a wisp of your breath. And yet you have called us to care for your creation. Help us to live in such a way that the threshing floors and the vats overflow with your mercy for all people. Help us to bring about the renewal of the earth as we return to you and once again live as your people.

Reflection

Creation Renewed

For you shall go out in joy, and be led back in peace; the mountains and the hills before you shall burst into song, and all the trees of the field shall clap their hands. Instead of the thorn shall come up the cypress; instead of the brier shall come . up the myrtle; and it shall be to the LORD for a memorial, for an everlasting sign that shall not be cut off.　　　—Isaiah 55:12–13

Meditation

There is perhaps no more exuberant image of the new creation than Isaiah's vision of God's redemption. When God makes all things new, the earth itself will rejoice. God's redeeming work is not only for the human part of creation, but for all of creation. The earth is returned to the harmony and interdependence for which God designed it; the new earth means a new relationship between humanity and the earth. Trees grow in place of thorns, flowers instead of tangled vines. The lush beauty of the Garden is restored, and the whole earth sings with joy.

Prayer

Oh God, how we await this day. We hold to your promise and trust in your faithfulness. We thank you for a vision of

what is to come and pray that you will help us to be part
of the healing and restoration you are bringing about
even now.

Reflection

For additional reflection on the topic of the earth, see the following subjects in The Green
Subject Index in The Green Bible: Agriculture, Covenant, Creator, Defile, Desert,
Desolation, Disobedience, Dust, Earth, Famine, Farm/Farmer, Field, Flowers, Food, Forest,
Fruit/Fruitful, Garden, Grain, Grass, Ground, Harvest, Land, Mountain, Plants, Pollution,
Property, Seasons, Soil, Trees, Wilderness, and World.

Water

I wish you could come here and rest a year in the simple unmingled love-fountains of God. You would return with fresh truth gathered and absorbed from pines and waterfalls and deep-singing winds, and you would find that they all sang of fountain love just as did Jesus Christ.

—John Muir (1838–1914),
  My First Summer in the Sierras

Water: The Sustainer

From the very first verse of Genesis to the very last chapter
of Revelation, images of water flow through the Bible with a
force that's hard to miss. In the Old Testament, water is a sign
of God's sustaining provision, of God's faithfulness, of God's
protection. In the New Testament, water becomes the sign
of new life, of redemption. Floods rage, rivers flow, rains fall
from the heavens—all reminders of God's continued activity
in the world.

It's not incidental that water carries these images of God as
the sustainer and renewer of life. Every living thing depends
on clean, fresh water for existence. Without water, orchards
and fields are barren, livestock suffer and die, cities crumble,
civilizations topple, whole nations of people die off. In the
ancient cultures of the Bible, there was no need to remind
people of their dependence on water; they were inextricably
tied to the cycles of rainy seasons and dry seasons. They
arranged their lives around the availability of water, building
cities along riverbanks, moving through the deserts to follow
the rain, planting and harvesting in accordance with the rain
patterns. Water as a sign of God's presence and provision,
as the source of life and therefore a gift to be cherished and
protected, would have been obvious to the Israelites of the
Old Testament.

Those of us who live in industrialized nations have gradually forgotten just how dependent we are on water. It flows freely from our taps. It keeps our lawns green and our food plentiful. When we want water, we have water. Yet its accessibility has led us to take water for granted. And while that has clearly led to a lack of care for the world's water supply, it has also led to a lack of connection between humanity and God. Water, this sacred element through which God has saved and protected God's people throughout history, has become meaningless to us. We have forgotten how to see the holy in the ordinary.

The passages in this section will guide you to a deeper understanding of the many ways water reflects God's image. Sometimes water is used as a metaphor for God's presence and sustaining power. Other times, water literally bears the healing and saving power of God. In every case, however, we find that God's fingerprint is present on the rivers, the seas, and the rain. When we protect the waters, when we are faithful stewards of this precious resource, we once again become mindful of God's creation. We return to the faith for which we were created: God living in and through our daily lives.

Explore: As you read these passages about water, pay attention to the ways God sustains you through your use of water throughout the day. You might even consider reading and meditating on these passages while sitting by a lake or a fountain where you can have a tangible sense of God's creative gift of water.

The Face of the Waters

And God said, "Let there be a dome in the midst of the waters, and let it separate the waters from the waters." So God made the dome and separated the waters that were under the dome from the waters that were above the dome. And it was so. God called the dome Sky. And there was evening and there was morning, the second day. And God said, "Let the waters under the sky be gathered together into one place, and let the dry land appear." And it was so. 　　　　　　　　　　　　　**—Genesis 1:6–9**

Meditation

From the very beginning of the story of God's activity in the world, water has been a force through which God has brought about life, God's glory has been made known, and God's people have been sustained and protected. Here, in the very first verses of Genesis, God moves over the waters, gathers the water into the seas, and uses the water to create life (see Gen 1:20–21). There is more here than mere symbolism. There is a vivid picture of God embedded in all that is created. From the vast seas to the smallest droplets of rain, God's creation—the water that flows over the surface of the earth and surges beneath its land—points us to God. In this most common element, the life-giving power of God is revealed.

Prayer

All-present God, you show us your glory in and through your creation. Open our eyes, renew our hearts, and teach us to recover the connection to you that we find through your creation.

Reflection

The Good Land

For the LORD your God is bringing you into a good land, a land with flowing streams, with springs and underground waters welling up in valleys and hills, a land of wheat and barley, of vines and fig trees and pomegranates, a land of olive trees and honey, a land where you may eat bread without scarcity, where you will lack nothing, a land whose stones are iron and from whose hills you may mine copper. You shall eat your fill and bless the LORD your God for the good land that he has given you.

—Deuteronomy 8:7–10

Meditation

This passage offers a stark contrast to the parched, barren desert in which the Israelites had wandered for forty years. God promises that the dust and death of the desert will be left behind as God's people move into the lush, living land where the waters rush, the vines are heavy with ripening fruit, and even the stones bring goodness and prosperity. This life, this bounty, is the symbol of God's faithfulness, the fulfillment of God's promise of deliverance. Water is at the heart of this blessing, this promise.

Prayer

Life-giving God, you bring us out of our dry days and into the valleys of life. Quench our pain with your sustaining love. Restore us with your flowing mercy. Renew us with the fresh hope of your goodness. Make us mindful of the life-sustaining blessings we too often take for granted.

Reflection

Dry as Dust

But if you will not obey the LORD your God by diligently observing all his commandments and decrees . . . The LORD will afflict you with consumption, fever, inflammation, with fiery heat and drought, and with blight and mildew; they shall pursue you until you perish. The sky over your head shall be bronze, and the earth under you iron. The LORD will change the rain of your land into powder, and only dust shall come down upon you from the sky until you are destroyed.   —Deuteronomy 28:15, 22–24

Meditation

Throughout most of human history—and indeed for much of the world today—rain means the difference between life and death; in agrarian cultures there is no greater fear than drought. Here, drought is a clear sign of God's anger, part of the long litany of afflictions that come with disobedience. Drought, illness, blight, and the misery they bring with them are the consequences of a people living out of sync with God and God's creation. As God's people move away from God, as they stop listening to God's call to live well with all of creation, the people suffer, and the earth does as well. The dry, barren, diseased earth is a sign of the broken connection between the people and their God. Even today, the actions of humanity and the state of the earth are tightly bound to each other. When creation is out of balance, when the streams are dry and the air is toxic, we are seeing the results of our own disobedience.

Prayer

Dear Lord, you rain down love and grace on us, and yet we fail to pay attention. We turn away, we look for false hope, we forget your goodness, and all of creation suffers for it. Help us to obey, to follow, to trust, and to attend to the never-ending goodness that pours from you each day.

Reflection

A Wellspring of Hope

When the water in the skin was gone, she cast the child under one of the bushes. Then she went and sat down opposite him a good way off, about the distance of a bowshot; for she said, "Do not let me look on the death of the child." And as she sat opposite him, she lifted up her voice and wept. And God heard the voice of the boy; and the angel of God called to Hagar from heaven, and said to her, "What troubles you, Hagar? Do not be afraid; for God has heard the voice of the boy where he is. Come, lift up the boy and hold him fast with your hand, for I will make a great nation of him." Then God opened her eyes, and she saw a well of water. She went, and filled the skin with water, and gave the boy a drink.　　　　　　　　　　**—Genesis 21:15–19**

Meditation

This is the story of Hagar, the mistress of Abraham, and her son, Ishmael. The two have been sent away by Abraham's wife, Sarah, and soon find themselves wandering the wilderness with no hope of rescue. When their small supply of water runs out, Hagar assumes their deaths are imminent and that they have been utterly forgotten by God. But God does not abandon this slave woman and her illegitimate child. God brings life and hope back to Hagar in the form of abundant water in the middle of nowhere. She has been cast out by her people, but through the life-giving water, God shows her she has not been forgotten. The water is her salvation, a gift from the God who loves her. Then—and now—God sustains the rejected as well as the righteous through God's glorious creation. In the same way, how can we provide water to the thirsty, to the Hagars in our world—the homeless, the poor, the outcasts? How can we be vessels of God's mercy?

Prayer

Merciful God, you embrace the rejected, fill the empty, sustain the desolate. You are the God of the outsider, the stranger, the castoff. You offer your life-giving presence and care to all who call on you. Make us vessels of your sustaining mercy. Show us how to be deep wells of compassion for all who seek your help.

Reflection

Reflection . . .

Presence and Protection

And he said, "Thus says the LORD, 'I will make this wadi full of pools.' For thus says the LORD, 'You shall see neither wind nor rain, but the wadi shall be filled with water, so that you shall drink, you, your cattle, and your animals.' This is only a trifle in the sight of the LORD, for he will also hand Moab over to you. You shall conquer every fortified city and every choice city; every good tree you shall fell, all springs of water you shall stop up, and every good piece of land you shall ruin with stones." The next day, about the time of the morning offering, suddenly water began to flow from the direction of Edom, until the country was filled with water.   —2 Kings 3:16–20

Meditation

The Israelites are heading into battle with the Moabites. But as they move toward enemy territory, they are without water. They see this as a sign that God is not with them as they proceed. The absence of water means the absence of God's sustaining power—they will lose strength quickly without water. But just as they are about to turn around, the prophet Elisha tells them that God will bring them water, without rain, and that they will have all they need to overtake the Moabites. And indeed, the next morning they wake up to find water everywhere—more than enough to sustain them and their animals through the battle ahead. Once again, water brings with it God's presence and protection. God's provision is seen and felt and known through the water God sends. How often do we take water for granted in our day? Yet without it we, too, suffer and lose strength.

Prayer

Loving God, you surround us with your protection, your care, your presence. You wash over us with mercy. You sustain us and redeem us with your unfailing love. Help us to trust that you are here, that you are with us and for us and in us, strengthening us in every way for whatever battles lie ahead.

Reflection

Reflection . . .

Abundant Love

You visit the earth and water it,
you greatly enrich it;
the river of God is full of water;
you provide the people with grain,
for so you have prepared it.
You water its furrows abundantly,
settling its ridges,
softening it with showers,
and blessing its growth.

—Psalm 65:9–10

Meditation

God's sustaining faithfulness is often demonstrated
through water. And yet God's love and care go far beyond
sustenance. The Psalmist speaks of abundant, overflowing
water that changes the earth as it moves over the face of the
land. This is not mere caretaking that keeps the earth alive.
It is bountiful, even excessive. Think of a careening stream,
a charging waterfall—the exuberant, playful rush of water
over rock that seems almost extravagant in its power and
beauty. God's transcendence expands beyond what we
imagine and alters us forever. As we reconnect with God,
God settles our rough places. God softens our parched

spirits. God blesses us and enriches us and makes us into more than we believed we could be.

Prayer

Abundant God, you are the giver of life and yet you give us so much more. Make us mindful of your generous love and care as you sustain us with water. Let us be changed by your glory. Like water settles the ridges of the earth, sculpt us and smooth us and soften us as you flow around us with your bountiful spirit.

Reflection

The Everlasting Promise

He will give rain for the seed with which you sow the ground, and grain, the produce of the ground, which will be rich and plenteous. On that day your cattle will graze in broad pastures; and the oxen and donkeys that till the ground will eat silage, which has been winnowed with shovel and fork. On every lofty mountain and every high hill there will be brooks running with water—on a day of the great slaughter, when the towers fall.

—Isaiah 30:23–25

Meditation

This prophecy comes after generations of rebellion from the nation of Israel. In the verses prior to this section of Isaiah, there is a long list of the ways in which the Israelites have rebelled against God. But at verse 18, the tone changes and Isaiah describes all the goodness God has in store for the Israelites. In many ways, this part of the prophetic promise echoes the language of Deuteronomy 8:1–7 where God tells the people about the good land that waits for them after their time in the desert. Here, those same visions of abundant rain, endless fields of grain, and flowing water from the mountains remind the people that God has not—and will not—abandon them. This promise is meant for us as well. When we find ourselves distant from God, when we fear that our rebellion and rejection have been too much, we find this assurance that God has not—and will not—abandon us. God continues to provide for us—through the rain, through the earth, through all of creation. We have God's everlasting promise.

Prayer

Dear God, when we turn from you, pull us back. When we close ourselves off from you, open us up. When we reject or ignore or try to push away from you, remind us that you are waiting for our return with all of the goodness and grace you have shown us from the beginning.

Reflection

Reflection . . .

The Power of Restoration

As I came back, I saw on the bank of the river a great many trees on the one side and on the other. He said to me, "This water flows towards the eastern region and goes down into the Arabah; and when it enters the sea, the sea of stagnant waters, the water will become fresh. Wherever the river goes, every living creature that swarms will live, and there will be very many fish, once these waters reach there. It will become fresh; and everything will live where the river goes. People will stand fishing beside the sea from En-gedi to En-eglaim; it will be a place for the spreading of nets; its fish will be of a great many kinds, like the fish of the Great Sea. But its swamps and marshes will not become fresh; they are to be left for salt. On the banks, on both sides of the river, there will grow all kinds of trees for food. Their leaves will not wither nor their fruit fail, but they will bear fresh fruit every month, because the water for them flows from the sanctuary. Their fruit will be for food, and their leaves for healing."   —Ezekiel 47:7–12

Meditation

This prophetic vision from Ezekiel pushes the idea of God's sustaining presence into a deeper place. Here, the water doesn't just sustain life, it brings life where there was none. With this water, life conquers death, abundance wins out over scarcity, and bounty replaces desolation. This passage hints at the New Testament and the coming of Jesus. There is a sense that something new is on the horizon, something that the people hadn't seen before—God as healer, restorer, and redeemer for all of creation. The water that will flow will do far more than maintain what was there. It will bring about something astonishingly new. Like the first blooms after a fierce winter, there is hope in this understanding of a restored creation. There are hints of this new earth all around us. Do you see them?

Prayer

Redeeming God, you bring life to the places we thought were dead—our barren souls, our hardened hearts, our shut-down spirits. You revive what has fallen still and dark. You bring fresh growth to the dying places in our lives. Give us hope. Give us faith. Give us eyes to see the tiny buds of life springing up in us.

Reflection

The Water of Life

Then Jesus came from Galilee to John at the Jordan, to be baptized by him. John would have prevented him, saying, "I need to be baptized by you, and do you come to me?" But Jesus answered him, "Let it be so now; for it is proper for us in this way to fulfill all righteousness." Then he consented. And when Jesus had been baptized, just as he came up from the water, suddenly the heavens were opened to him and he saw the Spirit of God descending like a dove and alighting on him. And a voice from heaven said, "This is my Son, the Beloved, with whom I am well pleased." —Matthew 3:13–17

Meditation

The sacrament of baptism is the symbol of purification and of being made a new creation in God. The use of water in the act of baptism harkens to the Old Testament stories of God's movement and activity through the waters—God moving over the water during the Creation narrative, the water bringing forth life, the water flowing through the Promised Land of the Israelites, the water arriving to fortify the Israelite army as it moved into Moab. In the sacrament of baptism, the use of water brings all of these stories together. As Jesus is baptized, he is marked as God's own Son, publicly anointed by God to be the fulfillment of God's covenant with creation. In Jesus, these other stories find their meaning. The redemption, healing, and restoration God promised and demonstrated through the waters throughout history is reflected as the waters wash over God's Son.

Prayer

Faithful God, the water that gave hope to your people in their darkest days continues to remind us of your great and unending love for us. Help us to be renewed each day by the promise of this love. Help us to be people who live out our baptism as we seek to be new creations.

Reflection

Reflection . . .

A Deeper Well

A Samaritan woman came to draw water, and Jesus said to her, "Give me a drink." (His disciples had gone to the city to buy food.) The Samaritan woman said to him, "How is it that you, a Jew, ask a drink of me, a woman of Samaria?" (Jews do not share things in common with Samaritans.) Jesus answered her, "If you knew the gift of God, and who it is that is saying to you, 'Give me a drink,' you would have asked him, and he would have given you living water." The woman said to him, "Sir, you have no bucket, and the well is deep. Where do you get that living water? Are you greater than our ancestor Jacob, who gave us the well, and with his sons and his flocks drank from it?" Jesus said to her, "Everyone who drinks of this water will be thirsty again, but those who drink of the water that I will give them will never be thirsty. The water that I will give will become in them a spring of water gushing up to eternal life." The woman said to him, "Sir, give me this water, so that I may never be thirsty or have to keep coming here to draw water." —John 4:7–15

Meditation

There is far more going on in this brief conversation than might be apparent at first. Jesus is making it clear that he is the continuation of the story that began back in the Old Testament, the story of God's ever-present love and care.

He is expanding the story by offering himself—the living water—to this Samaritan woman. She is from a race of people who would not have been considered part of God's covenant with the nation of Israel. On top of that, she was a woman with a reputation—she had been married several times and her appearance at the well at the hottest time of day suggests she was ashamed to be seen. But in this invitation to share a cup of water, Jesus is offering her—and everyone else who was thought to be beyond the covenant—the chance to be part of the story. Jesus uses the woman's understanding of the necessity of water to explain her need for spiritual sustenance. This is where we see the redemptive waters of Ezekiel's vision personified in Jesus. This woman is from the other side of the river, as it were. And now, as Jesus flows into her life, she too is invited to bear good fruit with the help of the living water of Christ. God's presence, God's grace and mercy, are there in the life-giving water that is Jesus.

Prayer

Our loving God, we are the next chapter of your ongoing story. We are invited to bear fruit that heals the world. Thank you for quenching us with the living water of Jesus. Embolden us today, to live out our part of the story.

Reflection

The Ultimate Revival

The name of the star is Wormwood. A third of the waters became wormwood, and many died from the water, because it was made bitter. . . . Then the angel showed me the river of the water of life, bright as crystal, flowing from the throne of God and of the Lamb through the middle of the street of the city. On either side of the river is the tree of life with its twelve kinds of fruit, producing its fruit each month; and the leaves of the tree are for the healing of the nations.　　　　　**—Revelation 8:11, 22:1–2**

Meditation

In the Revelation to John, the final book of the Bible, the great drama that has played out in the rest of the Bible depicts God's sustaining providence—and withering wrath—in water. In the first part of this passage, which comes in the midst of John's terrifying dream of destruction, the water has been tainted by evil and has become toxic. Where there was once life and promise, there is now only death and hopelessness. Water—the life-source of the people—has become their enemy. But John's vision brings back the hope—even harkening back to Ezekiel's language—as water once again demonstrates that God has not abandoned the people, even in the midst of great destruction (see Ezek 47:7–12). The river of the water of life, flowing out of the throne of God, brings with it the promise of God's continued love, restoration, and redemption for all of creation. As we look at the ways the earth's water has been tainted by human recklessness, we can hold on to this same hope: God is still here, renewing us and restoring all of creation.

Prayer

Dear God, you are our sustainer. You are our redeemer. You give us life. And you give it to us in abundance. As we see a reflection of your love in the water around us, may we never forget the promises you have made—promises of your presence, your care, and your great love for us. May we join you as you make all things new.

Reflection

Reflection . . .

For additional reflection on the topic of water, see the following subjects in The Green Subject Index in The Green Bible: *Drought, Famine, Rain, Renew/Restore, River, Seas, Storm, and Water.*

Air

All that is sweet, delightful, and amiable in this world, in the serenity of the air, the fineness of seasons, the joy of light, the melody of sounds, the beauty of colors, the fragrancy of smells, the splendor of precious stones, is nothing else but Heaven breaking through the veil of this world.

—**William Law (1686–1761),**
   Rules for Living a Holy Life

Air: The Life-Giver

Every human life that enters this world begins with the same dramatic act—a sharp intake of air. Our lungs fill for the first time and we become, suddenly, alive in a new way. Waiting parents listen for that first cry, the sign of health and life. The doctors watch the chest for the rise and fall that signals the passage of air in and out of the tiny airways. It is a tense moment, one heavy with expectation. A family's future hinges on the breath of a child.

The connection between breath and life is one that the nation of Israel understood in a profound way. The Hebrew word for breath is *ruach*, a word that also means "air, spirit, and life"—one word with layers of meaning. So when the Jews told the story of creation, of God bringing about life with a breath, they recognized that this act of breathing was God imbuing life with God's own Spirit. The breath of God carries the Spirit of God.

Breathing is so natural to us that we don't even think about it or consider the air around us. Yet the air God uses to bring about life is the same air that we have allowed to become threatening to life. In pollution-choked cities, children and the elderly are encouraged to stay indoors when the air quality becomes unsafe. We can't always see the toxic air, but when the act of breathing becomes labored, our bodies tell us that something is wrong, that the intended connection between human beings and the air around us has been disrupted. But we can repair that broken relationship by regaining our sense of God's connection to creation.

As you read the passages that follow, you'll see that the *ruach* words—*air, breath, life, Spirit*—are used throughout the Bible to express God's mark on every living creature, to demonstrate God's protection in the wind and the clouds, and to show God's renewing power in the Holy Spirit.

Explore: As you begin each devotional in this theme, take a moment to pay attention to your breath. Consider how each intake of breath fills you with a sense of God's calm and peace.

The First Breath

In the beginning when God created the heavens and the earth,
the earth was a formless void and darkness covered the face
of the deep, while a wind from God swept over the face of the
waters. —**Genesis 1:1–2**

Meditation

Genesis begins with this powerful image of nothingness.
There is darkness everywhere. There is the formless
void. And suddenly, God is breathing over the water and
bringing forth life. With this vital act, God begins the
amazing process of creation. The moon and the stars are
set in place, the sea and land and sky are teemed with
life, and human beings are charged with the privilege of
watching over it all. All of this creative work begins with
the breath of God. It's no wonder the Hebrew people
understood God's Spirit as a wind, a breath, the source of
all life. Without God's Spirit, there is nothing; with God's
Spirit there is vibrant being and abundant life.

Prayer

Creator God, you breathed and the earth was born. You
breathe and we have life. With each breath we take, remind

us of your goodness, your creation, and your charge to be the caretakers of all that you have made.

Reflection

The Breath of Life

Then the LORD God formed man from the dust of the ground, and breathed into his nostrils the breath of life; and the man became a living being.   —Genesis 2:7

Meditation

There is a little phrase in this passage that comes up several times in the Genesis account: *the breath of life* (see Gen 1:30, 6:17, 7:15, 7:22). At first, this seems like a simple way of thinking about the difference between life and death—a living thing breathes, a dead thing doesn't. But in the context of the Creation story that starts with the breath of God over the waters, this phrase takes on a richer meaning: Life begins when God breathes. When the phrase is used in the story of Noah (Gen 7:15), it is a reminder that humanity is not the only part of creation into which God breathed life. The breath of God becomes the mark of the Creator, and all of creation bears that mark—from the trees that provide us with oxygen to the animals that share our air.

Prayer

Loving God, the air we breathe keeps us alive. Every breath
is a gift from you. It is a constant reminder that you are
the source of life, the source of our breath. Help us to be
mindful of this gift and your life-giving spirit as we seek to
care for the life around us.

Reflection

Life Breath

The hand of the LORD came upon me, and he brought me out
by the spirit of the LORD and set me down in the middle of a
valley; it was full of bones. He led me all around them; there were
very many lying in the valley, and they were very dry. He said
to me, "Mortal, can these bones live?" I answered, "O LORD God,
you know." Then he said to me, "Prophesy to these bones, and
say to them: O dry bones, hear the word of the LORD. Thus says
the LORD God to these bones: I will cause breath to enter you,
and you shall live. I will lay sinews on you, and will cause flesh
to come upon you, and cover you with skin, and put breath in
you, and you shall live; and you shall know that I am the LORD."
So I prophesied as I had been commanded; and as I prophesied,
suddenly there was a noise, a rattling, and the bones came
together, bone to its bone. I looked, and there were sinews on
them, and flesh had come upon them, and skin had covered
them; but there was no breath in them. Then he said to me,
"Prophesy to the breath, prophesy, mortal, and say to the breath:
Thus says the LORD God: Come from the four winds, O breath,
and breathe upon these slain, that they may live." I prophesied
as he commanded me, and the breath came into them, and they
lived, and stood on their feet, a vast multitude.   —**Ezekiel 37:1–10**

Meditation

Like a second Genesis, Ezekiel's vision points again to the life-giving power of the breath of God. But this strange story reminds us that when God breathes life into creation, it is not just to fill the lungs. It is to bring life in its fullest sense. Without the breath of God flowing through us, we are like these dry bones scattered across the valley floor. We need God to fill us up, to give our lives meaning and purpose. The air around us is imbued with life-giving power. Breathe in the air and feel yourself expand with the fullness of life. Breathe in the breath of God and become truly alive!

Prayer

Father God, you are the giver of life. Fill us with the abundant life for which we were created. Expand us and strengthen us with the force of your breath. Make us more than flesh and bone. Make us people who are made alive by your sustaining love.

Reflection

A Towering Presence

The LORD went in front of them in a pillar of cloud by day, to lead them along the way, and in a pillar of fire by night, to give them light, so that they might travel by day and by night. Neither the pillar of cloud by day nor the pillar of fire by night left its place in front of the people.　　　　　—Exodus 13:21–22

Meditation

The Israelites had been enslaved for so long that their story had become one of oppression and captivity. Yet when at last they were free, they found themselves wandering through the desert. Any joy they felt at their release from Egyptian servitude must have been quickly replaced with a longing for food, shelter, and a place to rest. Yet God did not abandon them, but chose to lead them to a better life. The pillar of cloud was their guide and their protection during the day. The pillar of fire was their light and warmth at night. God chose to use those two pillars to make his presence known and to remind them that the Spirit of God, the *ruach* of God, is always here. So too should the life-embracing atmosphere give powerful witness to God's care of us in our day.

Prayer

Great God, we don't see you in pillars of cloud or towers of fire, yet we trust that you are with us. Forgive us for not acknowledging your presence. Help us to notice, to remember, to seek out, and to acknowledge your presence in the world around us. Show us your love in the everyday moments of goodness and grace in the air we breathe.

Reflection

God of the Air

Bless the LORD, O my soul.
O LORD my God, you are very great.
You are clothed with honor and majesty,
wrapped in light as with a garment.
You stretch out the heavens like a tent,
you set the beams of your chambers on the waters,
you make the clouds your chariot,
you ride on the wings of the wind,
you make the winds your messengers,
fire and flame your ministers.

—Psalm 104:1–4

Meditation

This beautiful poetic picture of God wrapped in light, riding on a cloud can almost distract us from the earthiness of the language the Psalmist employs. Here, God's majesty is connected to the most basic elements— wind, water, fire, light. There is no need for gold when there is God's own light to make a garment for God. There is no need for a mansion when there is the wide sea and the expanse of the heavens. There is no gilded chariot for the Almighty, but a cloud carried on the wind. God's creation expresses the glory and goodness of God. When we are seeking God, when we long for God, God's creation turns our eyes toward the One who made it all.

Prayer

Mighty God, open our eyes to the majesty of your creation. When we wonder where you are, draw us to you. Turn us from our need for proof and replace it with a vision of your presence in the world around us.

Reflection

Unseen Power

He stretches out Zaphon over the void, and hangs the earth
upon nothing. He binds up the waters in his thick clouds, and
the cloud is not torn open by them. He covers the face of the full
moon, and spreads over it his cloud. He has described a circle
on the face of the waters, at the boundary between light and
darkness. The pillars of heaven tremble, and are astounded at
his rebuke. By his power he stilled the Sea; by his understanding
he struck down Rahab. By his wind the heavens were made fair;
his hand pierced the fleeing serpent. These are indeed but the
outskirts of his ways; and how small a whisper do we hear of
him! But the thunder of his power who can understand?

—Job 26:7–14

Meditation

As Job responds to his friends, he can only imagine the
power God holds. And yet he stirs up these astonishing
images of God working in unseen ways that defy
explanation. At the same time, many of these images give
the sense of God moving in the air, through the wind,
with a breath. These are familiar ways of thinking about
God's activity in the world, and Job uses them to explain
the unexplainable. The ordinary points Job—and us—to
the extraordinary nature of God. Job finds comfort in these

pictures of God's power flowing through the air. He finds peace in this idea of God working behind the scenes and over the course of time. And because he trusts God, Job finds strength in the belief that God's activity is so much greater than he can ever know.

Prayer

Dear God, your creation is all around us, bringing about small wonders that we don't even notice. The mark of your creation is in the sound of thunder, in the rush of wind, in the boldness of lightning. Like Job, we seek your comfort, your peace, your strength as we rest in the knowledge of your greatness and power.

Reflection

Reflection . . .

A Voice in the Air

Six days later, Jesus took with him Peter and James and his brother John and led them up a high mountain, by themselves. And he was transfigured before them, and his face shone like the sun, and his clothes became dazzling white. Suddenly there appeared to them Moses and Elijah, talking with him. Then Peter said to Jesus, "LORD, it is good for us to be here; if you wish, I will make three dwellings here, one for you, one for Moses, and one for Elijah." While he was still speaking, suddenly a bright cloud overshadowed them, and from the cloud a voice said, "This is my Son, the Beloved; with him I am well pleased; listen to him!" When the disciples heard this, they fell to the ground and were overcome by fear. But Jesus came and touched them, saying, "Get up and do not be afraid." And when they looked up, they saw no one except Jesus himself alone. —Matthew 17:1–8

Meditation

God doesn't appear very often in the New Testament, but when God does, it is in this covering of a cloud. God uses the cloud—water particles suspended in air—as a protective barrier so Peter, James, and John would not be overwhelmed by God's glory, his *kabod*. God's divine presence is shielded from them by the thinnest of barriers in the covering of a cloud. For the Jews, this was God at his most intimate—a voice guiding them forward, showing them that the promise made to their ancestors was now fulfilled in Jesus. As we seek God's glory, we too can find that intimate connection to our Creator.

Prayer

Almighty God, we long for the day when there will no longer be a barrier to seeing you in your glory. Until that day, help us to magnify your glory here on earth by loving and caring for your creation well. Help us to recognize your voice, and to open our ears to your guiding presence.

Reflection

The Absence of Life

When he utters his voice, there is a tumult of waters in the heavens, and he makes the mist rise from the ends of the earth. He makes lightnings for the rain, and he brings out the wind from his storehouses. Everyone is stupid and without knowledge; goldsmiths are all put to shame by their idols; for their images are false, and there is no breath in them.

—Jeremiah 10:13–14

Meditation

This passage is striking not only for the ways in which Jeremiah uses nature to express God's power, but in the way he uses the life-breath of God as the distinguishing mark between what is real and what is false. There is life in the waters, life in the mists. There is power in the lightning, power in the wind. And yet the false gods have no power because they lack the breath of life. They lack the Spirit of God that flows from God's breath. In this sharp contrast, Jeremiah ties life, breath, power, and Spirit together as God's mark on creation. The world that God made stands in sharp contrast to the idols that human beings made. One is filled with God's goodness. The other, with human selfishness. If we want to live well with God, we must live well with the world God made.

Prayer

Gracious God, we are so often blind to your Spirit, immune to your presence. Help us to be people who see the mark of your creation in the wind and in the rain, in the air and in the clouds, in the life and in the light that surrounds us.

Reflection

God in the Storm

The LORD is slow to anger but great in power, and the LORD will by no means clear the guilty. His way is in whirlwind and storm, and the clouds are the dust of his feet. —Nahum 1:3

Meditation

For the ancient prophets like Nahum, the cycles of nature made for strong metaphors. If God's goodness was in the air, if God brought life to them with God's very breath, then it made sense for Nahum to speak of God's anger and wrath as a devastating windstorm. A whirlwind or dust storm could wipe out a crop, flatten a nomadic village, choke out livestock and children. It was a terrifying occurrence. What made whirlwinds particularly unsettling was that they came out of nowhere. Suddenly the dust would swirl up into the air and cover everything in its path with silt and debris. The unseen, unpredictable power of the wind was a recognizable picture of the potential wreckage that would come in the wake of God's anger toward the nation of Israel. Nahum uses descriptions from the natural world to point the people back to God—to remind them of God's power. If we are willing, these words can do the same for us.

Prayer

All-powerful God, you can churn the dust with your feet
and yet you speak to us in whispers of wind. Keep our eyes
open even when the world's dust threatens to blind us to
your glory. Help us to stand up in the storms we face and
seek you through the clouds that hover over us.

Reflection

The Life-Giving Spirit

When it was evening on that day, the first day of the week, and
the doors of the house where the disciples had met were locked
for fear of the Jews, Jesus came and stood among them and
said, "Peace be with you." After he said this, he showed them his
hands and his side. Then the disciples rejoiced when they saw
the LORD. Jesus said to them again, "Peace be with you. As the
Father has sent me, so I send you." When he had said this, he
breathed on them and said to them, "Receive the Holy Spirit. If
you forgive the sins of any, they are forgiven them; if you retain
the sins of any, they are retained."   —John 20:19–23

Meditation

When Jesus appeared to his disciples after his resurrection,
he brought them more than proof that he was indeed
alive—he gave them new life. As Jesus breathes on his
disciples, he is giving them the Holy Spirit. This is the
ruach, the breath, the life, the Spirit of God filling them
up and changing them. Something new is expected of
them in light of this Spirit. They are to be new people, new
creations. This act of breathing the Holy Spirit out brings
about new life for the disciples, one in which they follow a
resurrected Christ who is Life, who is Spirit, who is Breath.
With each breath, we too can take in the glory of God and

be reminded of the Spirit that fills us and sustains us and changes us.

Prayer

Merciful God, we breathe in your Spirit as the disciples did before us. May the life you give us extend to others as we forgive and seek to be forgiven.

Reflection

Born of the Spirit

What is born of the flesh is flesh, and what is born of the Spirit is spirit. Do not be astonished that I said to you, "You must be born from above." The wind blows where it chooses, and you hear the sound of it, but you do not know where it comes from or where it goes. So it is with everyone who is born of the Spirit.

—John 3:6–8

Meditation

This passage, part of Jesus' conversation with a Jewish leader named Nicodemus, connects the past to the present. Nicodemus comes to Jesus with the admission that he recognizes Jesus as one sent by God. As Jesus harkens to images of the wind and the Spirit, Nicodemus must have been reminded of the Creation narrative in which God breathes life into Adam. He must have thought about the *ruach* of God—the Spirit that brings life. And he must have understood that in Jesus, this Spirit was made flesh—that this man before him was indeed the Son of God, the embodiment of the Spirit. For a Jew like Nicodemus, the Spirit of God moved in and through history like the wind. And now, it stood before him. What an astonishing experience! The nuance of Nicodemus' experience tends to be lost on us because we have lost touch with that narrative of God moving in and through the air. But we can capture it again as we rediscover the God of the Hebrews who spoke and breathed on God's people.

Prayer

Father God, the air we breathe reminds us of your life-giving presence—the *ruach*. Help us to recognize and embrace the gift of your Spirit. Help us to notice how your Spirit creates new life in us each day.

Reflection

For additional reflection on the topic of air, see the following subjects in The Green Subject Index in The Green Bible: *Air, Cloud, Fire, Power, Sky, Stars, Storm, and Wind.*

Animals

If thy heart were right, then every creature
would be a mirror of life and a book of holy
doctrine. There is no creature so small and
abject, but it reflects the goodness of God.

—Thomas à Kempis (1380–1471),
   The Imitation of Christ

Animals: The Vulnerable

There is a profound symbiotic connection between human beings and the animals who share the earth with us. God created us to live in an interdependent relationship, in a cycle of life and death that would be mutually beneficial to both humanity and the animal kingdom. Over the course of history, human beings have depended on animals for food, transportation, work, income, health, and companionship. And animals have depended on human beings for protection, sustenance, and survival.

At times, the animal kingdom has suffered greatly because of human domination, abuse, industrialization, and simple ignorance. Yet we have also saved entire species from extinction simply by changing our understanding of what it means to live in this mutually dependent relationship. We wield tremendous power in our relationship with our fellow creatures, and the Bible is exceedingly clear on how we are to use that power.

God created the animal kingdom and declared it good. Then God handed over the care of this kingdom to human beings. The passages you will read in this section point to God's continual call for human beings to tend to other living creatures as God would. From God's tender request that Adam name the animals of the Garden to instructions for preparing an animal for sacrifice, God demonstrates deep concern for the creatures God has made. They are not treated casually by their Creator. They are known and provided for out of God's great love for all of creation.

Our dominion over the creatures who share this planet with us is a humbling call to serve and to protect, one that compels us to consider the ways in which our lives and our choices impact those creatures we are to care for.

Explore: As you read and meditate on the passages that follow, pray about one or two changes you could make in your daily routine that would demonstrate care or protection for the earth's animal populations—eating only free-range meats, volunteering with your local humane society, or reducing pollutants that impact local wildlife habitats.

God's Good Creation

And God said, "Let the waters bring forth swarms of living creatures, and let birds fly above the earth across the dome of the sky." So God created the great sea monsters and every living creature that moves, of every kind, with which the waters swarm, and every winged bird of every kind. And God saw that it was good. God blessed them, saying, "Be fruitful and multiply and fill the waters in the seas, and let birds multiply on the earth." And there was evening and there was morning, the fifth day. And God said, "Let the earth bring forth living creatures of every kind: cattle and creeping things and wild animals of the earth of every kind." And it was so. God made the wild animals of the earth of every kind, and the cattle of every kind, and everything that creeps upon the ground of every kind. And God saw that it was good. —Genesis 1:20–25

Meditation

Throughout the Creation narrative in Genesis 1, God declares each thing that is made to be "good." It's as though God is the artist finally standing back to look at his masterpiece, tweaking each feather, each leaf, each star, until the picture before him meets with the approval of his discerning eye. Each creature—each shimmering fish, each dazzling bird, each creeping insect—passes the test.

Each living thing that walks the earth or swims in the sea or flies through the air is declared good by the God who made it. It seems right, then, that we too see these creatures as the good creation of our God. How might it change the way we treat our earth and the animals who live on it when we consider them good?

Prayer

Creator God, we share this earth with creatures too numerous to name. And yet we pay them too little heed. Help us to see each animal as your creation, your good and perfect work of art.

Reflection

Reflection . . .

Dominion or Domination?

God blessed them, and God said to them, "Be fruitful and multiply, and fill the earth and subdue it; and have dominion over the fish of the sea and over the birds of the air and over every living thing that moves upon the earth." God said, "See, I have given you every plant yielding seed that is upon the face of all the earth, and every tree with seed in its fruit; you shall have them for food. And to every beast of the earth, and to every bird of the air, and to everything that creeps on the earth, everything that has the breath of life, I have given every green plant for food." And it was so.   —Genesis 1:28–30

Meditation

God's created order doesn't revolve around humanity alone. Here, after giving human beings the command to have dominion over all other living things, God demonstrates what that dominion should look like—and it doesn't look like domination or control. God points out the provisions for human sustenance—the seeds for planting, the fruit for harvesting—then adds that the animals have been given food as well. God has created the earth to sustain human life and animal life so that they are not competing for resources. God has made it clear that caring for these creatures will mean understanding the interdependence that exists in the human/animal relationship. It is left to the humans to maintain this delicate balance. Dominion, then, includes this element of care, of ensuring that the earth continues to provide for all living creatures, human and otherwise.

Prayer

Merciful God, we consume without consideration for the impact we have on those creatures we are called to care for. Forgive us for our recklessness in how we interact with your creation. Restore us to our place as caretakers of creation as we work to recalibrate the balance between human benefit and creation care.

Reflection

Reflection . . .

Created for Connection

Then the L<small>ORD</small> God said, "It is not good that the man should be alone; I will make him a helper as his partner." So out of the ground the L<small>ORD</small> God formed every animal of the field and every bird of the air, and brought them to the man to see what he would call them; and whatever the man called each living creature, that was its name. The man gave names to all cattle, and to the birds of the air, and to every animal of the field; but for the man there was not found a helper as his partner.

—**Genesis 2:18–20**

Meditation

It's interesting that in this second version of the Creation story, animals were created as partners for the man. It seems clear that God intended for humans and animals to live in some kind of interdependent relationship. There is an intimacy between the man and these animals—God brings each one to the man so he can name it, a request that suggests the man knows and understands each creature. And yet none of them make the right kind of partner for the man. There is no question that human beings are different from animals or that we connect with each other in ways we cannot connect with other living creatures. And yet, there is a connection that began in the Garden when God placed humans and animals together so that they could help one another. There is an interdependency that was ordained by God from the beginning.

Prayer

Loving Creator, our well-being is tied to the well-being of all creatures. Help us to recognize our dependence on the animals you placed in our care even as we accept their dependence on us. Make us gentle, compassionate, humane caretakers of these creatures and their environments.

Reflection

Reflection . . .

Re-created Creation

But I will establish my covenant with you; and you shall come into the ark, you, your sons, your wife, and your sons' wives with you. And of every living thing, of all flesh, you shall bring two of every kind into the ark, to keep them alive with you; they shall be male and female. Of the birds according to their kinds, and of the animals according to their kinds, of every creeping thing of the ground according to its kind, two of every kind shall come in to you, to keep them alive. **—Genesis 6:18–20**

Meditation

The story of Noah and the ark begins with God telling Noah that he is going to destroy the earth and everything on it because it has become too violent. Yet God isn't completely done with the earth. God asks Noah to save himself and his family. And then God asks Noah to save a pair of every living creature so that they will survive the coming destruction and be part of the new creation as well. In all of the turbulence surrounding this story, God remembers the animals. They are so essential to the created order that not a single species is to be left behind. Not one. The animals matter to God, and when they are not present, the balance of creation is lost.

Prayer

All-knowing God, the creatures with which we share the earth are not an afterthought for you. They are an intrinsic piece of the whole of creation. They are part of what makes the earth a reflection of your glory. Help us to protect and sustain them.

Reflection

A Matter of Life

Anyone who kills an animal shall make restitution for it, life for life. Anyone who maims another shall suffer the same injury in return: fracture for fracture, eye for eye, tooth for tooth; the injury inflicted is the injury to be suffered. One who kills an animal shall make restitution for it; but one who kills a human being shall be put to death.   —Leviticus 24:18–21

Meditation

There is tremendous violence and vengeance in this passage, so much so that it is one Jesus referred to when he spoke of turning the other cheek as a model of the new Law under Christ (see Mt 5:38–40). But in this passage we find not only a harsh understanding of retribution, but also a sense of the value of each living thing. While the punishment for killing an animal is not as severe as the price of killing a human being, there remains a need for restitution. The life of an animal matters to God, and it is not to be taken without cause. Other passages in Leviticus go into great detail about the proper way to care for animals given in sacrifice to God (see Lev 17:3–7). For God, there is nothing casual in the death of an animal. It is a matter that deserves attention, intention, and when necessary, restitution.

Prayer

Great God, you value each living thing. Teach us to be people who never kill for selfish gain, but who recognize the gift each animal is to us. And teach us to be a gift to them in return.

Reflection

God of the Details

Do you know when the mountain goats give birth? Do you observe the calving of the deer? Can you number the months that they fulfill, and do you know the time when they give birth, when they crouch to give birth to their offspring, and are delivered of their young? Their young ones become strong, they grow up in the open; they go forth, and do not return to them.

—Job 39:1–4

Meditation

This passage comes in the middle of God's long response to Job and his friends. In this response (which continues through the remainder of Chapter 39), God reminds Job that it is God who created each living thing, that it is God who watches over the earth and all that God made. But what's beautiful about this proclamation is the intimacy of God's knowledge. This isn't the voice of a distant overseer. Rather, it is the voice of the one who made each living thing. God speaks of the smallest details of these creatures' lives—when they give birth, what they eat, where they sleep, their flying patterns. It is a reminder to Job that God is a God of details, of the small moments, that God pays attention to the first steps of a deer and to the nest of the eagle. The animals are not held up as superior to humans

(Job 39:9–12 is all about the ox as an animal meant for work). Instead, they are examples of the fullness of God's care for all of creation—human being and animal alike.

Prayer

Almighty God, you are not a removed Creator but one who is in and around every detail of creation. Help us to honor your presence and faithfulness by being graceful and grateful partners in caring for the earth and all of the creatures in it.

Reflection

The Cost of Connection

How long will the land mourn, and the grass of every field wither? For the wickedness of those who live in it the animals and the birds are swept away, and because people said, "He is blind to our ways."
—**Jeremiah 12:4**

Meditation

We are created to live in interdependence with other living creatures. We depend on animals, fish, birds, and insects for our food. We use animals to help us with our work, we use them to fertilize our crops, to keep us company as pets. Our dependence is clear. And yet all living things depend on human beings as well. When we live in such a way that we change the earth's environment, other living creatures suffer. This isn't a new problem. Jeremiah uses this interdependence as a warning to the nation of Israel—their sin will change the earth. It will leave the fields dry and withered. It will drive away and kill off the animals and birds. Human sin trickles down into all of creation, leaving devastation everywhere it goes.

Prayer

All-powerful God, you see all that we do, for we know you are not blind to our ways. Forgive us for the selfish choices we make that damage your creation. Help us be agents of restoration and renewal. Heal the earth and the creatures who live on it. Bring us new life as you redeem all you have made.

Reflection

The Lesson of the Sheep

The word of the LORD came to me: Mortal, prophesy against
the shepherds of Israel: prophesy, and say to them—to the
shepherds: Thus says the LORD God: Ah, you shepherds of Israel
who have been feeding yourselves! Should not shepherds feed
the sheep? You eat the fat, you clothe yourselves with the wool,
you slaughter the fatlings; but you do not feed the sheep. You
have not strengthened the weak, you have not healed the sick,
you have not bound up the injured, you have not brought back
the strayed, you have not sought the lost, but with force and
harshness you have ruled them. So they were scattered, because
there was no shepherd; and scattered, they became food for
all the wild animals. My sheep were scattered, they wandered
over all the mountains and on every high hill; my sheep were
scattered over all the face of the earth, with no one to search or
seek for them.   —Ezekiel 34:1–6

Meditation

As we have seen, the words of the prophets are often
metaphors from nature. In this passage, Ezekiel uses
the image of a lazy, self-centered shepherd to scold the
people of Israel for failing to care for one another. It's a
powerful image because these agrarian people would have
immediately understood the steep cost of the shepherd's

actions. They knew that the sheep depended on their shepherd for everything, while at the same time providing him with his livelihood. If they scattered or died off, he would suffer as well. As we consider what it means to care for animals as part of God's creation, Ezekiel's words almost lose their metaphorical sense and become literal. We have clothed ourselves and fed ourselves at the expense of others—people and creatures. We have neglected to care for the vulnerable—people and creatures. And as a result, we have hurt ourselves. Like lazy shepherds, we have let the creatures in our care die off on our watch. But we can wake up and return to the work God has given us. We can step back into the interdependence that God intended from the beginning.

Prayer

All-knowing God, we have been negligent, leaving unattended all those whom you have placed in our care. Change us, move us, alter us so that we follow your path, the path of our Good Shepherd and care for the poor, the vulnerable, the needy parts of your creation.

Reflection

God's Provision

Therefore I tell you, do not worry about your life, what you
will eat or what you will drink, or about your body, what you
will wear. Is not life more than food, and the body more than
clothing? Look at the birds of the air; they neither sow nor reap
nor gather into barns, and yet your heavenly Father feeds them.
Are you not of more value than they? And can any of you by
worrying add a single hour to your span of life? And why do you
worry about clothing? Consider the lilies of the field, how they
grow; they neither toil nor spin, yet I tell you, even Solomon
in all his glory was not clothed like one of these. But if God so
clothes the grass of the field, which is alive today and tomorrow
is thrown into the oven, will he not much more clothe you—
you of little faith?   —Matthew 6:25–30

Meditation

This well-known verse reminds us to let go of worry and
trust in God's provision. But it also tells us something
about God's care for the earth. Even the lowliest sparrow
is fed by the hand of God. Even the wild lilies are touched
with the beauty of their creator. God cares for the smallest
and least significant parts of the earth. It is our calling as
God's people to do the same.

Prayer

Gracious God, thank you for being our provider. Continue to show us how our presence can make a difference, even among the least of these. Help us to protect and care for all of the earth's inhabitants with the grace and attention you show to us and to all of your creation.

Reflection

Under God's Care

Are not two sparrows sold for a penny? Yet not one of them will fall to the ground apart from your Father. And even the hairs of your head are all counted. **—Matthew 10:29–30**

Meditation

The sparrow appears again as Matthew uses these tiny birds to make a point: God is a God of details. Matthew is trying to help his audience see God as a God who cares deeply about humanity. But this message only works when we understand how much God cares for even the creature that seems the most worthless. Because God *does* notice the fallen sparrow, we are assured that God notices us as well. When we consider what God's call of dominion means, this should be our model: To notice, to care, to protect, and to defend. To be moved when animals are harmed by human activity and to do something about it. That is what we as God's people—the keepers of the earth—were created to do.

Prayer

Our Great God, nothing escapes your notice. Help us to notice too. Make us people of compassion who see the fallen bird, the ravaged field, the dying species as you do.

Reflection

Redemption for All

The wolf shall live with the lamb, the leopard shall lie down with the kid, the calf and the lion and the fatling together, and a little child shall lead them. The cow and the bear shall graze, their young shall lie down together; and the lion shall eat straw like the ox. The nursing child shall play over the hole of the asp, and the weaned child shall put its hand on the adder's den.

—Isaiah 11:6–8

Meditation

Our faith teaches us that God will restore all of creation. There will be a new heaven *and* a new earth. The mark of this new earth is described in this passage from Isaiah, giving us a beautiful picture of the healed relationships between all created beings. Animals that once lived as enemies will live together without strife or fear of death. The animals that became the enemies of humanity as the result of sin will no longer threaten us or fear us. God's restoration, God's redemption, extends to all of creation. Each creature lovingly created by God and cared for within the dominion of human existence will be part of the new earth promised in the Bible. As we work to bring about this kingdom, we can begin by taking our role as caretakers of the earth to heart and protecting the creatures with which we share the earth. In doing so, we are part of God's continual effort to bring about the new earth here and now.

Prayer

Redeeming God, we wait for the day when all of creation is healed and made new. Make us agents of change as we seek your kingdom and the redemption that is waiting for us all.

Reflection

For additional reflection on the topic of animals, see the following subjects in The Green Subject Index in The Green Bible: *Animals, Beasts, Birds, Creatures, Dominion, Fish, Insects, and World.*

Humanity

The first law of our being is that we are set in a delicate network of interdependence with our fellow human beings and with the rest of God's creation.

—Desmond Tutu (1931–),
   God Has a Dream

Humanity: The Caretakers

Conversations about creation care typically center on the planet—the air, the water, the land—and the protection of animals. And yet at the heart of creation care sits a human rights issue, one we too often ignore. Creation care isn't just about caring for the earth. It is about caring for one another. Human beings are also a part of God's beloved creation.

Nearly every human struggle comes back to the earth in some way. Wars have been fought over land, oil, water, access to ports, or control of shipping routes. A lack of food and water leads to rebellion and strife for numerous countries. Infants die for the lack of clean water. Whole tribes of people are decimated over a drought or restricted water supply. We cannot care for our fellow human beings without caring for the earth. Even if we find no other case for creation care compelling, we ought to be changed by this one.

The passages you will read and meditate on in this section center on the biblical truth that human beings are created in the image of God. If we genuinely believe that God created humanity to carry that image, to live as God's people on the earth, then caring for one another becomes nonnegotiable. The connection that so many of us have yet to make, however, is that protecting the environment is a means of caring for our brothers and sisters around the world. Our sin and pride has distorted our view of clean water as a political bargaining chip rather than a life-and-death issue for huge portions of the world's population. Clean air is not code for reining in business; it is one of the keys to global health. Reducing consumption means freeing up resources for poor nations. These are acts of justice, of restoration. They are reflections of the work of our Creator whose image we bear.

This is the interdependence God intended for human beings—that we protect one another, care for one another, and love one another. When he was asked which commandment was most important, Jesus named two: To love God and to love our neighbors as ourselves (see Mk 12:29–31). We cannot do one without doing the other. The most meaningful connection within all of creation is that connection between human beings. Created for relationship, we are nothing without one another. It is in our care for one another that we reflect God's care for us. Together, we are the image of God.

Explore: Seeking justice for the poor and oppressed can seem overwhelming. As you read these passages, pay attention to the ideas and inspirations the Holy Spirit gives you. Follow those leanings to find ways you can be part of God's healing work in the world.

The Image of God

Then God said, "Let us make humankind in our image, according to our likeness; and let them have dominion over the fish of the sea, and over the birds of the air, and over the cattle, and over all the wild animals of the earth, and over every creeping thing that creeps upon the earth." So God created humankind in his image, in the image of God he created them; male and female he created them.   —**Genesis 1:26–27**

Meditation

In all of creation only one part bears the image of God: humanity. This image is not one of isolation or individualism. It is one of relationship—"male and female he created *them*." Neither the man nor the woman bears the image alone. It takes both of them, two people in a relationship, to reflect God's image. If we look even deeper into this passage, we find that the charge of dominion also bears the image of God. Our care for the earth, our care for one another, is to reflect God's care for us. This reciprocal relationship between God, humanity, and the whole of creation puts us in a place of extraordinary privilege. We are the image bearers when we care for all of God's creation in the way of our Creator.

Prayer

Life-giving God, you have imbued us with your image and asked us to carry it well, mirroring your love for the world. Forgive us for the ways we have failed to reflect your love and care. Compel us toward lives of mercy, compassion, and justice so that we might be worthy of bearing your image.

Reflection

The Justice Connection

For six years you shall sow your land and gather in its yield; but the seventh year you shall let it rest and lie fallow, so that the poor of your people may eat; and what they leave the wild animals may eat. You shall do the same with your vineyard, and with your olive orchard.   —**Exodus 23:10–11**

Meditation

The first part of Exodus 23 exhorts the nation of Israel to work for truth and justice in their legal proceedings. Then comes this set of rather odd farming instructions. But the connection is clear: justice is not limited to the law; it is an everyday expectation of God's people. It is so crucial that even their use of the land needs to reflect God's longing for justice and care for the poor (see also Lev 19:10 and Deut 24:19–21). The land with its fields and vineyards and orchards is a means of bringing about justice for the poor and oppressed. In caring for the land, God's people are caring for each other.

Prayer

Dear God, we are people of plenty, and yet so many have nothing. Our earth offers a rich bounty, more than enough for all of us and yet too often we seek only to provide for ourselves. Turn us around, Lord. Show us the faces of the poor and give us hearts of compassion. Help us to obey you and respond.

Reflection

The Requirements of Justice

You must not distort justice; you must not show partiality; and you must not accept bribes, for a bribe blinds the eyes of the wise and subverts the cause of those who are in the right. Justice, and only justice, you shall pursue, so that you may live and occupy the land that the LORD your God is giving you.

—Deuteronomy 16:19–20

Meditation

Themes of justice and caring for the poor come up several times in Deuteronomy (see especially Deut 15:11). Here, the need for God's people to seek and practice justice and care for each other is tied directly to their journey to the Promised Land. Justice in the form of concern for the poor and fair dealings with all people are so important to God that God is prepared to deny them what they long for most—a land of their own. Perhaps God wants them to realize that unless they become people of justice and mercy, of care and compassion, living in the Promised Land will be just as miserable as living in captivity. True freedom comes from living out our calling as God's people. To oppress one another with injustice, bribery, and partiality means we have traded one form of enslavement for another. God's promise of a better life only becomes reality when we live as better people.

Prayer

Lord God, teach us to be people who pursue justice. Help us to cultivate mercy and to care for one another in your name. Reform us as we seek to be your people.

Reflection

The God of Justice

Happy are those whose help is the God of Jacob,
whose hope is in the LORD their God,
who made heaven and earth,
the sea, and all that is in them;
who keeps faith forever;
who executes justice for the oppressed;
who gives food to the hungry.
The LORD sets the prisoners free;
the LORD opens the eyes of the blind.
The LORD lifts up those who are bowed down;
the LORD loves the righteous.
The LORD watches over the strangers;
he upholds the orphan and the widow,
but the way of the wicked he brings to ruin.

—Psalm 146:5–9

Meditation

So many of the Psalms focus on the majesty of God, on God's power and might. But here, the Psalmist praises God's care for the poor, God's justice on behalf of the oppressed. The God celebrated here is not removed from human suffering. This God is intimately connected with the people God made. This is the God who feeds the hungry and sets free the imprisoned. This God, the God who created the expanses of the heavens and the depths of the sea, cares for the hurting and the lost. This is the God in whose image we are made.

Prayer

Merciful God, you are Lord of the universe and yet you care for the poorest among us. You see those who are hurting. You bring hope to those who lost hope long ago. Because of our connection to one another, when one of us suffers, we all suffer. Help us restore humanity by caring for those among us who are in pain. Give us eyes to see. Make us people of justice.

Reflection

Reflection . . .

Redemptive Restoration

Is not this the fast that I choose: to loose the bonds of injustice, to undo the thongs of the yoke, to let the oppressed go free, and to break every yoke? Is it not to share your bread with the hungry, and bring the homeless poor into your house; when you see the naked, to cover them, and not to hide yourself from your own kin? Then your light shall break forth like the dawn, and your healing shall spring up quickly; your vindicator shall go before you, the glory of the LORD shall be your rear guard. Then you shall call, and the LORD will answer; you shall cry for help, and he will say, Here I am. —Isaiah 58:6–9

Meditation

The Bible is one continuous narrative of the goodness of creation, the brokenness that comes to all of creation through human sin, and God's efforts to restore creation to wholeness. This passage is a microcosm of that narrative. The people of the nation of Israel often practiced fasting through worship. Isaiah, however, tells them that their worship has no meaning unless it leads them to care for one another. Their own suffering is tied to the suffering they have ignored in others. But when they practice justice, when they clothe the naked and house the homeless, they too are restored. Harmony, peace, renewal only come when all of creation is living in an interdependent, connected relationship for which it was made.

Prayer

Oh God, we long to be restoration people, to be agents of redemption and healing. Turn our focus off of our own brokenness and need and show us where we can restore one another.

Reflection

The Least of These

Then he will say to those at his left hand, "You that are accursed, depart from me into the eternal fire prepared for the devil and his angels; for I was hungry and you gave me no food, I was thirsty and you gave me nothing to drink, I was a stranger and you did not welcome me, naked and you did not give me clothing, sick and in prison and you did not visit me." Then they also will answer, "LORD, when was it that we saw you hungry or thirsty or a stranger or naked or sick or in prison, and did not take care of you?" Then he will answer them, "Truly I tell you, just as you did not do it to one of the least of these, you did not do it to me." And these will go away into eternal punishment, but the righteous into eternal life.　　　　　—Matthew 25:41–46

Meditation

With this powerful story, Jesus takes God's call for justice to an even deeper place. Caring for the poor, feeding the hungry, healing the sick are not options when we understand that all human beings bear the image of God. All human beings share the same *ruach*, the life-giving Spirit that God breathed into humanity at the dawn of creation. To ignore the needs of other people is to ignore the image of God in them. It is to reject the connection and relationship for which we were created. It is to reject the one who created us.

Prayer

Gracious God, you have chosen us to bear your image and called us to care for your creation. Forgive us for being so focused on our own needs that we have forsaken the needs of a stranger. We have let our brothers and sisters go hungry. We have turned away from the poor and oppressed. Change us. Move in our hearts, so that we may extend your love, mercy, and grace to those in need.

Reflection

Global Justice

Just then a lawyer stood up to test Jesus. "Teacher," he said, "what must I do to inherit eternal life?" He said to him, "What is written in the law? What do you read there?" He answered, "You shall love the LORD your God with all your heart, and with all your soul, and with all your strength, and with all your mind; and your neighbor as yourself." And he said to him, "You have given the right answer; do this, and you will live." But wanting to justify himself, he asked Jesus, "And who is my neighbor?" Jesus replied, "A man was going down from Jerusalem to Jericho, and fell into the hands of robbers, who stripped him, beat him, and went away, leaving him half dead. Now by chance a priest was going down that road; and when he saw him, he passed by on the other side. So likewise a Levite, when he came to the place and saw him, passed by on the other side. But a Samaritan while traveling came near him; and when he saw him, he was moved with pity. He went to him and bandaged his wounds, having poured oil and wine on them. Then he put him on his own animal, brought him to an inn, and took care of him. The next day he took out two denarii, gave them to the innkeeper, and said, 'Take care of him; and when I come back, I will repay you whatever more you spend.' Which of these three, do you think, was a neighbor to the man who fell into the hands of the robbers?" He said, "The one who showed him mercy." Jesus said to him, "Go and do likewise."   —Luke 10:25–37

Meditation

In this parable of the Good Samaritan, perhaps one of
the best-known stories in the Bible, Jesus lays out what is
perhaps the least-followed command in the Bible: to love
our neighbor. The shock of Jesus' story has been lost on
us, but to his listeners, there was no more reviled ethnic
group than the Samaritans—mixed-ethnicity people were
not considered real Jews by other Jewish tribes. The twist
in Jesus' story is that it is this Samaritan—the seemingly
godless enemy—who acts out God's love and care. To
love our neighbor means to live as global citizens. It is to
understand ourselves as part of a larger picture in which
we seek for others the same goodness we seek for ourselves.
As Jesus makes clear, this kind of love is not based in being
right or being strong or being wealthy. It is based in mercy,
in reaching out with grace even to those we perceive as
enemies, even to those who perceive us as enemies. It is to
work for an end to injustice and oppression on behalf of all
the people God created, not just the ones most like us. This
is the essence of justice and creation care.

Prayer

God of grace and mercy, replace our fear with compassion,
our hatred with love, our anger with peace, our inaction
with care. Make us good neighbors who recognize your
image in all people.

Reflection

The Goodness of Humanity

For the one who sanctifies and those who are sanctified all have one Father. For this reason Jesus is not ashamed to call them brothers and sisters, saying, "I will proclaim your name to my brothers and sisters, in the midst of the congregation I will praise you." And again, "I will put my trust in him." And again, "Here am I and the children whom God has given me." Since, therefore, the children share flesh and blood, he himself likewise shared the same things, so that through death he might destroy the one who has the power of death, that is, the devil, and free those who all their lives were held in slavery by the fear of death. For it is clear that he did not come to help angels, but the descendants of Abraham.   —Hebrews 2:11–16

Meditation

We often hear humanity spoken of as depraved, broken, inherently sinful—straying far from the first Garden, destroying creation's gifts. We also know that human beings have the capacity to care both for each other and for the earth. The writer of Hebrews makes the case that we share a heritage with Jesus—we have one Father—and we are all called his brothers and sisters. We share not only this divine connection, but the earthly connection as well. Jesus was fully human. God chose the human form as the embodiment of his Son. Our value in the eyes of our Creator could not be greater. Our humanity is not something to be scorned or reviled. It is what makes us most precious to God. And it is this precious humanity that we are called to celebrate and honor in others.

Prayer

Faithful God, you came to us in human form to redeem us and to help us to see you as you see us—holy, beloved, and good. Help us to see your holiness in one another. Help us to honor your creation and care for your beloved children. Help us to be the good people you created us to be.

Reflection

A Chosen People

But you are a chosen race, a royal priesthood, a holy nation, God's own people, in order that you may proclaim the mighty acts of him who called you out of darkness into his marvelous light. Once you were not a people, but now you are God's people; once you had not received mercy, but now you have received mercy.

—1 Peter 2:9–10

Meditation

Here, Peter is giving a call to the people. It is a rallying cry meant to inspire them to see themselves as more than who they are. Like any good leader, Peter wants to bring out the best in those around him. And so he reminds them of who they are, of where they came from, of who created them and why. *We* are this chosen race. *We* are the royal priesthood that has been called into God's marvelous light. There is great responsibility with this calling, but God has filled us with the Spirit and placed God's stamp of approval on us. We are the recipients of God's great mercy through Jesus, and we are charged with proclaiming this mercy throughout the world. This is what marks us as God's people. It is a terrifying call. But it is also a call for which we have been equipped by our Creator. By showing us endless love, God has filled us with love. By

showing us endless grace, God has filled us with grace.
By showing us endless mercy, God has filled us with
mercy. We are to pour all that we have been given out on
our fellow human beings. This is creation care.

Prayer

Loving God, make us worthy of the priesthood you have
bestowed upon us. Help us reflect your marvelous light
in word and deed as we seek to be people of mercy and
justice.

Reflection

God's Dwelling with Renewed People

Then I saw a new heaven and a new earth; for the first heaven and the first earth had passed away, and the sea was no more. And I saw the holy city, the new Jerusalem, coming down out of heaven from God, prepared as a bride adorned for her husband. And I heard a loud voice from the throne saying, "See, the home of God is among mortals. He will dwell with them; they will be his peoples, and God himself will be with them; he will wipe every tear from their eyes. Death will be no more; mourning and crying and pain will be no more, for the first things have passed away."   —Revelation 21:1–4

Meditation

So often, the language we use for God pushes God out of our human experience. We tend to speak of God as something other—remote and distant. But here, in John's vision of the new Jerusalem, God is fully present. God is with us, living in and among the people. The healed, restored earth is home for us and for our God. This grand renewal places human beings as living with God, partnering with God as he always intended for us to do. This is where God is leading us, to a life in which all of humanity is restored to its essential, God-given goodness in a magnificently renewed creation. And humanity, God's

greatest creation, shares a dwelling place with the Most
High God.

Prayer

Almighty God, we ache for this new creation, for the day
when you restore us and walk among us as you once did in
the Garden. We have strayed so far from that place and yet
you too work for the day when all will be healed and we
will once again walk together. Help us to be part of your
work, of your redemptive activity in the world.

Reflection

*For additional reflection on the topic of humanity, see the following subjects in The Green
Subject Index in The Green Bible: Bless/Blessing, Caring for Your Neighbor, Community,
Covenant, Food, Humans, Justice, Life/Live, People, Poor, and Power.*

Stewardship

Let everyone regard himself as the steward
of God in all things which he possesses. Then
he will neither conduct himself dissolutely,
nor corrupt by abuse those things which God
requires to be preserved.

—John Calvin (1509–1564),
Commentary on Genesis

Stewardship: The Calling

All that God created, from the heavens to the seas, was created as a reflection of God's glory. If we have eyes to see and ears to hear, we can recognize God's creation in the air around us. We can see God's provision in the food we eat and the water that sustains life. We can connect to God as we care for one another.

The call to have dominion over creation is not a call for domination. It is a call to see God in the world around us and to know that we alone have been chosen to care for what God made. We are God's partners in caring for creation. And we will be God's partners in renewing creation as God brings about the new heaven and the new earth.

There is great hope in that vision, and yet we seem to have lost sight of that hope. It has been replaced with efforts to tame nature, to control it, to make it work for us while never really understanding that we cannot work without it. We have exhausted and abused what God created—all out of ignorance as well as selfishness. We have spoiled the land, rerouted the waters, filled the air with chemicals, driven entire species to extinction, and left millions and millions of our brothers and sisters to live in squalor and scarcity so that we can have more. But when we recover that hope, when we reclaim our place as caretakers of God's creation, we can once again be part of what God is doing in the world. Jesus taught us that to follow him means to be servants, not masters (see Mk 10:45). For too long, we have lived as the masters of creation. Yet our calling is to be people who serve, who tend, who nurture. That calling extends to what God had placed in our care.

The passages in this theme can be damning indictments of the long history of human selfishness and rebellion against God. But they also point us to that hope that God has always been about making all things new and that our sin has never stopped God from bringing about God's kingdom here on earth. This is what stewardship means. It is to partner with God as God cares for creation and uses creation to care for us. It is to respond to God's calling that we tend to the fields and flocks. It is to arrange our lives so that we are not people who control creation but those who seek to live well with what God made.

Explore: During the next readings, reflect on how God's call to care for the earth might change how you live or think about creation. What steps do you want to take to live well with God and all that God has made?

The Call to Care

The LORD God planted a garden in Eden, in the east; and there he
put the man whom he had formed. Out of the ground the LORD
God made to grow every tree that is pleasant to the sight and
good for food, the tree of life also in the midst of the garden,
and the tree of the knowledge of good and evil. . . . The LORD
God took the man and put him in the garden of Eden to till it
and keep it.   —Genesis 2:8–9, 15

Meditation

From the very beginning, humanity has been charged with
the stewardship of the earth—the Hebrew word in Genesis
2:15 is *abad*, which means "serve." Serving and caring for
creation is not an option for those who seek to follow God.
It is what we were created to do. This calling suggests that
as we tend to the earth, as we tend to one another as God's
creation, we are following God's first command. Creation
care becomes an act of worship, an act of obedience and
service—not of the earth but of the one who created the
earth. God called us into partnership from the moment we
were brought into being. We are God's hands and feet on
the earth, the caretakers of all God has made.

Prayer

Glorious Creator, thank you for the gift of this earth, for
the trees, for the flowers, for the animals, for the stars
and the seas and the sky. Thank you for entrusting us with
the responsibility of loving, serving, and caring for your
creation. Out of our great love for you, help us to restore
what has been degraded. Help us to be the caretakers you
created us to be.

Reflection

The Cost of Sin

And to the man he said, "Because you have listened to the
voice of your wife, and have eaten of the tree about which I
commanded you, 'You shall not eat of it,' cursed is the ground
because of you; in toil you shall eat of it all the days of your life;
thorns and thistles it shall bring forth for you; and you shall eat
the plants of the field. By the sweat of your face you shall eat
bread until you return to the ground, for out of it you were taken;
you are dust, and to dust you shall return." —**Genesis 3:17–19**

Meditation

The partnership and interdependence that God designed as
intrinsic to creation came to a quick end when sin entered
the picture. The selfishness of humanity not only changed
our relationship with God, it changed the relationship God
intended for us to have with the rest of creation. Instead
of there being a harmonious connection between human
beings and the rest of the earth, there would now be work,
stress, labor, pain, decay. The famine, drought, and other
natural disasters that were to come were not part of the
original plan. They were the result of a broken relationship,
a broken partnership. We continue to live under the cloud
of enmity between human beings and nature. Because this

break came as a result of human sin, it will take human effort to repair the damage.

Prayer

Redeeming God, we ask forgiveness for the brokenness we have brought into the perfect partnership you intended for your creation. Help us to heal what we have wounded and to restore what we have damaged.

Reflection

Moving Toward Restoration

If you follow my statutes and keep my commandments and observe them faithfully, I will give you your rains in their season, and the land shall yield its produce, and the trees of the field shall yield their fruit. Your threshing shall overtake the vintage, and the vintage shall overtake the sowing; you shall eat your bread to the full, and live securely in your land. And I will grant peace in the land, and you shall lie down, and no one shall make you afraid; I will remove dangerous animals from the land, and no sword shall go through your land. —**Leviticus 26:3–6**

Meditation

Passages like this one are often used to suggest that if we live a certain way, God will bless us with material possessions and economic prosperity (see also Deut 6:18; 28:1, 9–10; 30:8–10, 16). But that's not what God is talking about here. Instead, this passage is God's effort to restore what was lost in the Garden. Obedience doesn't bring prosperity; it brings harmony, balance, interdependence. This is a vision of what God intended all along—fertile fields and bountiful harvests. This is not something that we earn, but what we are intended to recover as we once again follow the path God laid out before us. It is what comes from living out God's call to stewardship. It is a picture of the new earth.

Prayer

Father God, thank you that you have called us to be partners in building your kingdom and that we are part of your plan for creating a new heaven and a new earth. We see glimpses of your renewal and new birth in your cleansing rains and overflowing fields. Bless us as we obediently work to recover what we once lost.

Reflection

The Meeting Place

Surely his salvation is at hand for those who fear him,
that his glory may dwell in our land.
Steadfast love and faithfulness will meet;
righteousness and peace will kiss each other.
Faithfulness will spring up from the ground,
and righteousness will look down from the sky.
The LORD will give what is good,
and our land will yield its increase.
Righteousness will go before him,
and will make a path for his steps.

—Psalm 85:9–13

Meditation

This is what partnership with God looks like. God's love
meets our faithfulness. God's righteousness meets our
efforts to live in peace. God gives us what we need and
we are able to heal the earth so it once again brings forth
goodness. This ancient poetry still resonates with us today
as we ache for this same moment, the one in which righteousness and peace kiss each other. But that kiss calls
for us to move forward, to press toward God and live out
God's command of stewardship. As we care for creation, we
are being obedient to that call. We are practicing the kind

of faithfulness that springs from the ground and meets God's steadfast love in a perfect embrace.

Prayer

Wonderful God, your love and faithfulness surround us in the air we breathe, in the water that nourishes the earth, in the people who care for us. May your Spirit prompt us to meet you in the place of partnership. Move us into action as we live out the call to righteousness and faithfulness.

Reflection

Reflection . . .

A Picture of the Present

The earth shall be utterly laid waste and utterly despoiled; for the LORD has spoken this word. The earth dries up and withers, the world languishes and withers; the heavens languish together with the earth. The earth lies polluted under its inhabitants; for they have transgressed laws, violated the statutes, broken the everlasting covenant. Therefore a curse devours the earth, and its inhabitants suffer for their guilt; therefore the inhabitants of the earth dwindled, and few people are left.　　—Isaiah 24:3–6

Meditation

It's stunning to consider that these words, written thousands of years ago, still speak to us today. Isaiah's vision of a ruined earth hints at the environmental damage around us now as we see entire continents battle ongoing drought, air laced with toxic fumes, and thousands of people dying each day because they lack clean water. What was once prophetic hyperbole is now reality. The broken earth has suffered because of human greed, human selfishness, human oppression. Our long-standing failure goes beyond driving big cars or using plastic bottles. It stems from a long-lost sense of our calling to be caretakers of what God created. Clearly, our generation is not the first to fail in this calling—Isaiah is talking to the nation of

Israel here—but we are a generation that can step toward God instead of away. We can be part of the new creation instead of continuing to desecrate the old.

Prayer

Forgiving God, you created us as your partners in caring for creation. In your mercy, forgive us for our failure to live out that calling and for the devastating results that have followed. Help us to step back into this partnership and stem the tide of our actions. Help us to heal the world we have broken and to save the lives we have ignored. Strengthen our resolve and give us renewed hope that when we follow your lead, there is nothing we cannot do.

Reflection

Reflection . . .

A Land of Horror

But my people have forgotten me, they burn offerings to a delusion; they have stumbled in their ways, in the ancient roads, and have gone into bypaths, not the highway, making their land a horror, a thing to be hissed at forever. All who pass by it are horrified and shake their heads. —**Jeremiah 18:15–16**

Meditation

The sins of humanity—greed, self-interest, corruption, oppression—have indeed led to a land of horror. We don't always see the results of this sin here in the West, but the nations that have been on the receiving end of centuries of abuse, slavery, and domination at the hands of the powerful know just what these horrors look like. The disease, famine, pollution, and war that threaten our brothers and sisters around the world are the result of humanity forgetting the path of stewardship God set before us, and wandering the byways of power and wealth instead. But when we acknowledge our carelessness, when we reclaim the calling God has given us, we can change the downward spiral of horror. We can be part of God's efforts to bring health, freedom, renewal, and peace to the most desperate among us.

Prayer

Oh God, we so often fail to focus on those who truly pay the price for human selfishness. We admit that it's easier to turn the other way. Give us the courage to stand up for the most vulnerable, for those who don't have the resources to recover. May we be mindful of our fellow human beings who suffer each day the catastrophic consequences of human sin.

Reflection

Creation Restored Through Care

For I am about to create new heavens and a new earth; the former things shall not be remembered or come to mind. But be glad and rejoice forever in what I am creating; for I am about to create Jerusalem as a joy, and its people as a delight. I will rejoice in Jerusalem, and delight in my people; no more shall the sound of weeping be heard in it, or the cry of distress. No more shall there be in it an infant that lives but a few days, or an old person who does not live out a lifetime; for one who dies at a hundred years will be considered a youth, and one who falls short of a hundred will be considered accursed. They shall build houses and inhabit them; they shall plant vineyards and eat their fruit. They shall not build and another inhabit; they shall not plant and another eat; for like the days of a tree shall the days of my people be, and my chosen shall long enjoy the work of their hands. They shall not labor in vain, or bear children for calamity; for they shall be offspring blessed by the LORD—and their descendants as well. Before they call I will answer, while they are yet speaking I will hear.   —Isaiah 65:17–24

Meditation

Isaiah's foretelling of the new creation offers a stunning sense of what life will be like when the earth is restored— the end of illnesses that kill the most vulnerable, the end of slavery and oppression, the end of fear and destruction. All of this is tied in to creation care, justice, and stewardship. As people care for the earth, they are able to care for one another. As people care for one another, they care for the earth. Resources and people are not disposable. They are part of this glorious new Jerusalem.

Prayer

Great God, we ache for the day when all is restored, when the whole of creation is healed from the consequences of our sin. Strengthen us as we work toward that restoration. Show us how to be part of your healing work in the world. Thank you for the hope of what is to come.

Reflection

Reflection . . .

True Stewardship

Hear the word of the LORD, O people of Israel; for the LORD has an indictment against the inhabitants of the land. There is no faithfulness or loyalty, and no knowledge of God in the land. Swearing, lying, and murder, and stealing and adultery break out; bloodshed follows bloodshed. Therefore the land mourns, and all who live in it languish; together with the wild animals and the birds of the air, even the fish of the sea are perishing. **—Hosea 4:1–3**

Meditation

Our calling as caretakers of the earth goes far beyond taking shorter showers or helping protect the rain forests. Stewardship involves a comprehensive change in how we live with God and one another. Hosea's prophecy ties human sin to the destruction of the earth. But that sin isn't only a disregard for the earth and other people, it's a disregard for God. The interdependence God wove into creation is disrupted whenever we stop living the lives God intended for us—lives in which we care for creation and creation cares for us. Recovering our calling to creation care means turning once again to the God who created us so that we live as the peacemakers, the caretakers, the stewards of all that God made. When we are right with

God, we will make choices that lead to a healed, renewed earth.

Prayer

Dear God, we have been unfaithful, disloyal, and forgetful. Thank you that we were created by you, a loving God who made us to live in harmony with the world around us. Help us return to that harmony as we repair damaged relationships, damaged communities, and the damaged earth.

Reflection

The Spirit of Stewardship

By contrast, the fruit of the Spirit is love, joy, peace, patience, kindness, generosity, faithfulness, gentleness, and self-control. There is no law against such things. And those who belong to Christ Jesus have crucified the flesh with its passions and desires. If we live by the Spirit, let us also be guided by the Spirit. Let us not become conceited, competing against one another, envying one another. —**Galatians 5:22–26**

Meditation

Imagine what the earth would be like if we all practiced these fruits of the Spirit. Because we are created by God, because all of humanity was imbued with God's Spirit at Creation, because we are called to live as God's people in the world, we are to bear these fruits. When we do, it becomes impossible to do damage to our brothers and sisters around the world. We cannot be people of peace while creating strife for others. We cannot be people of self-control when we are only thinking of our own interests. When we seek to be people who live out the fruit of the Spirit, we simply cannot do anything but live as God intended.

Prayer

Gracious God, tend to us so that we might produce your good fruit. Turn over the hardened soil of our hearts and bring back the rich ground in which your Spirit can thrive. Help us to live as your people.

Reflection

The New Covenant

This is the covenant that I will make with the house of Israel after those days, says the LORD: I will put my laws in their minds, and write them on their hearts, and I will be their God, and they shall be my people.
                                                                    —Hebrews 8:10

Meditation

There can be a tendency to lose hope when we look at the earth and consider all the ways in which humanity has strayed from God's call to stewardship. And yet God has never lost hope. God has never given up on us. God's covenant with his people has always been one of new life, new creation, a new heaven, and a new earth. That covenant has never been cast aside. God is here, bringing about God's kingdom on earth. We have only to join in. When we see ourselves as part of what God is doing in the world and work to participate with God in the healing of the world, we find that our hope is healed as well.

Prayer

God of Hope, it is a blessing to be your partners in renewing the earth. We are humbled and grateful for your faith in us. Help us to have that same steadfast faith in you

as we reclaim your call to be connected with all of creation.
May your kingdom come on earth as it is in heaven.

Reflection

For additional reflection on the topic of stewardship, see the following subjects in The Green Subject Index in The Green Bible: Covenant, Creation, Disobedience, Dominion, Humans, Judge/Judgment, Obedience, Prayer, and Stewards/Stewardship.

If you enjoyed
The Green Bible Devotional,
you might also love The Green Bible

Discover the Bible's powerful message for the earth.

Available wherever books are sold

Visit www.greenletterbible.com
for more information on how to get involved.

HarperOne
An Imprint of HarperCollins*Publishers*
www.harperone.com